Born With The Power To Win

Ayo Olaseinde

Clink Street

Published by Clink Street Publishing 2022

Copyright © 2022

First edition.

ISBN:
978-1-915229-33-5 - paperback
978-1-915229-34-2 - ebook

This book is dedicated to my mother, Edith Martha Olaseinde.

She taught me the price of love and the price of commitment. She taught me how to deal with disappointment and failure, how to smile in the face of adversity, and how to be an optimist. She gave me great principles and values to live by, and that has been the foundation of my success.

I still hear your voice… You are the best mother in the world… I Love You.

My determination for success was to make sure the sacrifices you made for your children were not in vain.

We love you and miss you.

I would like to thank my father for his discipline. Also, for teaching me how to be an optimist, and for my Christian upbringing.

My children, Joshua, Hannah, and Lisa; for their love, support, putting up with me and for being my inspiration. You are the best; I love you.

CHAPTER ONE

A time for change

It was Saturday afternoon. I had just dropped my wife, Isabella and our twin boys, Emilio and Jason at Manchester airport and I was headed home. It was a wet and gloomy spring day and I couldn't help but think how miserable my life had become. I started to feel sorry for myself and negativity creeped in. How did I get here? How did I get into this mess? This can't be what life is all about, one problem after another. Where have all the smiles gone? Why me? I asked myself. What have I done that is so bad to make me deserve all of this? I'm sick and tired of struggling; in fact… I'm sick and tired of being sick and tired. What am I going to do? There must be a way out of this mess. If only I knew how to get myself out of this predicament I'm in. I just seem to be stuck in a rut. Maybe it's my fault… Maybe it's me? Maybe I'm destined for a hard life? It's just not fair! I was having my own little pity party. I felt as though my life was so much harder than everyone else's. Just then, the heavens opened, and an avalanche of hailstones fell from the sky. The little angry pellets of ice bounced off the car. 'That's just great,' I said out loud. 'Have you got anything else you want to throw at me?' I muttered. 'Why me? Why does everything have to happen to me?' I stopped at a red traffic light, looking at the red light, I thought it reflected my mood. 'I wish I could magically change the lights, so I could get home quicker and out of this awful weather, it's making my mood worse.' I watched as a discarded carrier bag blew across the road, with no clear direction, just being tossed around by the wind. I feel just like that bag, I have been tossed around. Then lightning suddenly flashed across the sky. 'Perfect,' I thought, with a great deal of sarcasm.

***

It had been an especially tough week at work and at home. Why is it that when things are going badly at work, they are difficult at home as well? For the past few weeks, Isabella and I had been arguing about finances, the kids had been playing up, but the final straw was last night. Isabella was in tears; I was ready to throw the towel in and walk out. I just couldn't take it anymore. I knew she was right about us living beyond our means but my pride, or should I say of what little pride I had left, was knocked out of me. I could not even support my family by paying for the budget airline fares so that my wife and kids could go to Spain and visit her mum and dad. I felt embarrassed and humiliated. I was brought up with the belief that the man of the house, the husband, should be able to take care of his family, but this was something that I am failing at miserably.

Isabella and I had been together since our college days. I remember the first time I laid eyes on her. I had bumped into her in the canteen. Literally. I wasn't watching where I was going and we collided. I had a chocolate milkshake in my hand, and it ended up all down the front of her dress. As I looked up to apologise, I was mesmerised. She had long chestnut hair, falling in curls around her shoulders. Her eyes were the colour of emeralds lined with thick dark lashes. There was a smattering of freckles on her nose. I was lost for words. I had fallen for her in an instant. The rest, as they say, is history. How I wish we could turn back the time and revisit those days. Instead, life happened. Kids happened, and as the worries and stresses of money – or should I say the lack of it, ate into our existence, I had forgotten to appreciate her. I know I have taken her for granted on occasions, but it isn't all my fault. It's down to circumstances that are out of my control

Isabella's parents paid for the flights, they also offered to pay for me. I overheard Isabella on the phone telling her mum how we were strapped for cash, so her mum said that she would buy the tickets as a gift, but I made my excuses and said that I couldn't get the time off work. Humiliation washed over me. I have never been comfortable with accepting what I deem to be handouts. We haven't been able to afford a family holiday for such a long time. Isabella's mum and dad have helped us out a couple of times when bills have landed on the doorstep, with those horrible words in red: FINAL DEMAND.

***

If only I had got that promotion and pay rise. That would have helped, but they gave the job to Andrew. I needed it more than he did. It's not fair, I mean, life isn't fair is it? I continued with my own character assassination all the way home.

The stormy weather had started to lift too, and the clouds were starting to part so that the sun could finally peek through.

I passed the supermarket on the way home and decided to call in and treat myself to a couple of bottles of red wine. Isabella had done the shopping before she left, but we were on such a tight budget, that all alcohol had been banned from the house. I had an extra £20 that I had hidden from Isabella. She wasn't going to be home for a week. What she doesn't know won't hurt her, I reassured myself.

As soon I got through the front door I opened one of the bottles. I threw some logs into the wood-burning stove and got the fire going. I sat down in my favourite armchair and stared at the fire. I watched the flames flickering, deep in thought about my situation. It had grown dark now; the street lights had come on and shone a little beam of light into the living room, complementing the fire. I was really feeling sorry for myself. 'Why me? There must be a way; I have to find a way out of this mess,' I repeatedly told myself.

Things were going great until I got made redundant three years ago. I was out of work for almost six months, and by the time I had landed myself a new job, we were in arrears with our mortgage and up to the limits on the credit cards. Red text headed letters were a daily occurrence. We were living above our means, but nobody knew except for Isabella and her parents. I inwardly cringed with shame and took another mouthful of wine.

Most of our arguments were money-related. I think it must be my ego. I didn't like Isabella telling me what to do, I felt like she was constantly nagging and nagging. Isabella wanted to use her hairdressing qualification, and go to work part-time whilst the twins were at school so that we would have a bit of extra income but I wouldn't hear of it. I'm supposed to be the breadwinner, the man of the house. I just needed to make more money to get us out of this mess. I felt an emotion of both anger and sadness. Was this my destiny? Is this it? Is this my life? I continued to stare into the fire, my mind drifting when I heard a voice. I'd heard the same voice several times over the past year but tonight it sounded much clearer, then I heard the voice again saying:

'Michael, Michael stop persecuting and feeling sorry for yourself.' I jumped up as it felt as though I was no longer alone in the room. 'Who's there?' 'Who's there?' I said as I scanned the room nervously. There were no lights on, just the silhouette from the fire and the streetlight.

Then I heard the voice again: *'Michael, I have come to help you.'*

My heart was now pounding, had I left the front door open? I jumped up and put the lights on as I began to check the rest of the house, testing all the doors as I went. The house was empty. The doors were locked.

I sat back down in the chair. It was now 8 pm and I had been sitting in the living room for the last couple of hours. I hadn't mentioned this to anybody, but I had been hearing this voice calling my name over the past year. 'Am I losing my mind?' I thought to myself. *'No you are not losing your mind,'* said the voice. *'I have been calling you for the past 12 months. When are you going to stop and listen to me?'*

My heart was now pounding even harder than before. I looked around, I couldn't see anyone. Had all this stress finally taken its toll on me? Had I started to lose my marbles? I looked into the fire, and the flames appeared to have changed colour. There were still the oranges and yellows flickering, but now there were shades of pink and violet dancing around the hearth. All of a sudden I felt a warmth inside of me and an overwhelming feeling that everything was going to be all right. I just knew that I needed to listen to the voice instead of blocking it out as I had done before.

'Who are you?' I asked, not expecting to get an answer. *'Who are YOU Michael, that is the question?'* 'I know who I am, I'm Michael' I said. 'Who are you?' I exclaimed, this time with more assertion. *'Are you just a name Michael, or are you more than a name? Does your name describe who you are?*

Who you really are? What you like or dislike in people, life and love. Does your name explain your character? What you stand for and believe in. Michael, you are so much more than a name.' I paused for a moment and thought; what an interesting way of looking at yourself. I said out loud – I guess I AM more than a name, but you still haven't told me who you are.

There was a pause. *'I am not a name, who I am is for you to decide. What I am is your connection to the universe; a force for good, a higher power, your conscience. You can call me whatever you like. I can be the solution to all your problems. I am here to help. I have Ten Steps to reveal to you that will help change your life, but first, you must promise me four things. Firstly, you must listen, without interruption to what I have to say. Secondly, I want you to learn from these teachings that I am going to impart to you. Thirdly, you must apply the information I am about to give you. Finally, the fourth thing, I need you to share this newfound knowledge with others. Can you promise me all four Michael?'*

I thought for a few moments and said, 'I don't know If I have the courage or self-confidence to do that. I suppose it depends on what the Ten Steps are.' *'Michael, why do you doubt yourself? You can do whatever you want to do, you were born to win. Do you think I would be giving you these steps if I wasn't convinced you could handle them? You can do it, I know you can, but ultimately the choice is yours.'*

I thought about this for a few seconds, but it felt like much longer. My heart rate began to slow down and I began to feel a sense of inner peace. I wasn't afraid anymore. For the first time in ages, I began to smile. It IS my choice I said out loud. I'll do it, what have I got to lose?

'You possibly have a lot to lose Michael,' said the voice. *'I can read your thoughts. You could lose ten, twenty, thirty, forty, fifty+ years of happiness and fulfilment if you don't do something starting right now. You don't want to lose all these years of happiness, do you?* **Is your life worth fighting for?**

'Life is a journey. The question is… are you prepared to take control of that journey? So, Michael, it is now decision time… what will it be? You asked for help and now the help is here.' This time I didn't hesitate, I knew what I had to do. 'I am ready for the Ten Steps' I said.

'Will you promise to listen, learn, apply and share the Ten Steps?' 'Yes, yes, I promise to listen, learn, apply and share!' I replied without delay.

Today is a new start in my life. I felt a new energy, the adrenaline was flowing. It was like I had been plugged into the universe. It was at that moment, when I remembered an old saying that I had read in one of the motivational books that I used to read, but were now gathering dust on the bookshelf; **'When the student is ready, the teacher will appear'**. I was desperately ready

I grabbed a notepad and a pen so that I could write everything down that I was about to learn. The voice spent the entire evening giving me the Ten Steps. I wrote all night long. As dawn broke and the birds began to sing, my hand ached from writing. The voice spoke for the final time.

'Michael, many call for my help but only a few give me the chance to help them. Knowledge is only powerful when you use it. I will not speak again, but I will be watching. The Ten Steps are yours to use and share. Please use them wisely.'

I got up and checked the fire, but it had completely gone out. I looked at my watch. I had been listening and writing non-stop for over ten hours. I was emotionally and physically drained and yet I felt relaxed and content. There was a serenity about me. I'd never felt like this before. I rubbed my tired eyes, got up from my armchair, and made my way up the stairs to bed, with an overwhelming sense that everything in life is going to be alright. I fell into a deep sleep and was abruptly woken around 2 pm to the sound of my phone ringing. I quickly got up and I thought to myself; 'Was it all a dream, or did the Ten Steps really happen to me?' Just then, I saw my notebook; I grabbed hold of it and started to read a few pages.

It was true; I couldn't put the book down. The phone rang again. It was Isabella. *'I've been calling, didn't you hear your phone?'* 'Sorry,' I said, 'I was outside washing the car'. I didn't know what made me say that, but I felt that I couldn't tell Isabella about my experience. Not yet, anyway. We talked for a few minutes and after we said our goodbyes, I immediately went back to the Ten Steps.

I spent the rest of the day and evening, quietly going over the Ten Steps and completing the exercises. I felt good about life. The future was bright, but I couldn't help hearing the last few words the voice had said to me, being repeated over and over again in my mind. *'Many call for my help but only a few give me a chance to help them.'* I was one of the few. I felt humbled and so glad that I had finally listened.

The voice had also said to me, *'Knowledge is only powerful, when you use it.'* I had done my Ten Steps but I needed to make sure that this newfound excitement was going to lead to action and my action plan would begin tomorrow. **'I am born to win,' I said out loud with a huge grin on my face. I made myself some supper, drank the last bit of wine from the bottle, and had an early night.**

***

It was a Monday morning, my alarm went off at 7 am as usual. I jumped out of bed with extra vigour and went into the bathroom. As I looked in the mirror I said out loud, 'This is a new day, a new opportunity. A start of a new me. Today is going to be different.' I couldn't wait to get to work to tell Ade, my best friend, about my experience and the Ten Steps.

Ade and I had been friends for a few years, and we got along like a house on fire. He was tall and slim, his skin a russet, reddish-brown, and had hazel eyes which shone with a boyish charm when he smiled. Ade wouldn't think I had gone a bit bonkers – listening to a voice that gave me advice. No, he was very open-minded and was very easy to be with. He's considerate and understands other people's problems well, and above all else, he's honest.

As I drove to work, I had a big smile on my face. The sun was shining It has been years since I looked to the future positively. The first ten minutes at work was interesting. The first few people I met at work asked me; *'Why are you so happy? Have you won the lottery?' 'No!' I replied, 'I've got something that works better than the lottery.'* They were naturally intrigued and wanted to know more, but I kept tight-lipped about the details of my newfound enlightenment.

I worked in a small office which was primarily a sales and service business. There were about fifteen of us that worked there. As lunchtime arrived, Ade and a few of my colleagues came over to my desk.

'Come on Michael, tell us. What have you got that's worth more than a lottery win, go on tell us?' 'Are you sure that you really want to know?' I said. *'Yes we are!'* they said in unison. I couldn't keep it to myself anymore. I decided to tell them a shortened version of my previous night's encounter. I explained about the voice and the Ten Steps; 'But I can only share these steps with you if you are at the point in your life that you want to change and take control. You have to be committed to listening, learning and applying these steps.' They looked at me, and then at each other. I could see that they were sceptical about what I was saying.

'You have been reading too many of these motivational books,' said Tom. I felt myself getting slightly annoyed and I clenched my hands. I recalled in my mind what the voice had said to me: *'Many call for my help but only a few give me a chance to help them.'* How can you help someone who doesn't want to be helped? How can you help someone when they are in denial about their situation? 'Right guys, I said, I'm starving, I need to get some lunch. You can laugh if you want,' and I got up from my desk to go to the sandwich shop. I was not going to let this bunch of people laugh at my thoughts and beliefs. I wasn't going to let their attitude bring me down from the high I was feeling. I also had once been a doubting Thomas. But from now on I was no longer going to be sceptical and negative.

Ade put his hand on my shoulder, looked me in the eye and said, 'Michael, I don't doubt for one minute that something happened to you over the weekend, you seem like a new man. I haven't seen you this animated for such a long time now. Whatever it is that you have experienced, I'm so happy for you.'

Ade, Tom and Brianna followed me out to the shop to get a sandwich. *'We're sorry Michael',* Brianna said; *'I thought that you were joking, but I can see how serious you are about this. Did it really happen the way you said it did?'* 'Yes it did,' I said with a little more edge to my voice than I normally would have. 'Ade, you know how I have been feeling lately, and we have been friends for long enough to know that I would never make up a story like this. The voice is one thing that I can't explain completely for you to get your head around, but the Ten Steps make so much sense. I have already started the change. You see the problem is, **some people get to a point in their lives, when they become so sceptical, they cannot see the solutions to their problems**. They just see problems. I know this only too well, as that is the way I have been living my life up to this point. But no longer.'

'Michael, I want to know more about the Ten Steps!' said Ade *'So do I,'* said Brianna and Tom. 'There is a condition attached to revealing the Ten Steps and that is, once you start, you must complete all the steps and exercises. Don't pass judgement before you have done all Ten Steps for yourself. I looked at my watch and saw that it was time to get back to work, I said to the guys, 'Have a really hard think about what I have told you and let me know your thoughts later on. If you want to go ahead and start on the journey to a better you and a better life, we can do it tonight; but don't forget that you need to be 100% committed. This is different, this is special. The choice is yours, but I will tell you one thing, it has given ME vision, newfound energy and a feeling of purpose again.'

I was even beginning to sound like the voice!

It was about 4 pm in the afternoon when Ade and Brianna came over to my desk. Ade said *'We have both decided that this is a fantastic opportunity to try something new, we are committed and we believe in you Michael. We just don't understand the voice bit, but we both have open minds and are ready to get started straight away!'* 'What about Tom?' I said. Brianna looked down at her feet and shuffled them slightly before looking up *'Erm he thought about it and decided that he hasn't got the time, but let me be honest with you he also said that he just thinks it's a load of nothing anyway. He doesn't believe in visions or anything of that nature'*

'I wouldn't call it a vision, but more of a connection to a higher intelligence,' I said .*'We don't feel like Tom, we want to do it.'* said Ade. 'It's ok, I know that not everyone feels like they believe they could do the Ten Steps – I guess some people just don't think it's for them' I replied.

'When you are ready, your inner thoughts will let you know this: "When the student is ready, the teacher will appear." Unfortunately, we live in a world where some people expect miracles to solve their problems, not simple everyday solutions.'

'This reminds me of a story I once heard about a great flood.'

'As the flood worsened, everybody had been evacuated, except for this one man who wouldn't leave his home. The water was rising fast, the ground floor and first floor were completely submerged. He sat on the roof of his soon to be underwater home when some rescue workers in a rowing boat saw him. As they went to his rescue, the man refused their help, saying; *"I am a Christian and I believe in God. The good Lord will save me. I have lived in this house for fifty years and I am not leaving."* The rescue workers' efforts to coax the man from the roof were in vain so they decided to leave. The water was still rising, and the man was now on top of the chimney when he was spotted by a rescue helicopter. The helicopter lowered and threw a set of rope ladders down. Using a megaphone, the rescue workers shouted; *"Grab the ladders and climb up, we will save you!"* The man replied; *"No, I am a Christian, I believe in God, the good Lord will save me. I was born in this house and lived in this house for fifty years and I am not leaving. The good lord will save me."* They couldn't convince him either so they flew off.

'The water continued to rise and the man drowned.

'He woke up in heaven, as the man was a good man. When he realised where he was, he was raging with anger. He had put all his faith in God and God had done nothing. He saw St. Peter at the gates of heaven and asked him *"Where is my Lord?"* Peter pointed in the direction to which the man should take. When he stood in front of God, he said; *"God, my Lord, I have been your faithful servant for fifty years. When the great floods came, I asked for your help. I believed that you would come to my rescue, but you failed me. Why did you fail me lord?"*

'God paused for a second, looked him straight in the eyes and said; *"My son, my son, I did not fail you. I sent a rowing boat to rescue you, I sent a helicopter to rescue you, and you turned them away. What were you expecting, a miracle?"*

'You see the moral of the story is; **our solutions to our problems do not come in the form of miracles. They come as everyday solutions**. That is what the Ten Steps are all about, practical solutions. Most people never understand this because they are looking for miracles.'

'I love the story,' said Ade, *'... it's just so true; I suppose I am like that myself'*

'Well I am glad you are on board. Let's meet tonight at the Rose & Crown, does 7 pm suit you? I'll buy the drinks, so long as you promise to come with an open mind. Oh, and don't forget to bring a pen and notepad.'

As Ade and Brianna walked back to their respective desks, I thought to myself, 'Why did you offer to buy the drinks when you can't afford it? I'm going to have to take control of myself.' I was just excited and I couldn't help but think this was my first opportunity to share what I had learned. I had never done this before. I needed to go over my notes again and prepare.

I left work at 5 pm on the dot. As I drove home, I felt a rush of energy as I thought about what was going to happen this evening. I looked in the freezer and selected one of the meals that Isabella had prepared for me before she left for Spain. She knew that I would probably just go for an easy and unhealthy option if left to my own devices. As I heated it through, I read my notes. The more I read the clearer and more confident I became. I knew this was the way forward. I ate my dinner, washed the dishes and then I grabbed my wallet. I checked I had my credit card in there – it was almost maxed out, but a few drinks wouldn't break the bank I told myself.

***

I got to the pub just before 7, and Brianna was the first to arrive. I hadn't had anything to do with Brianna outside of work, but she had a really friendly personality and everyone seemed to like her. She was small in stature, with strawberry blond hair cut in a neat bob and I guess she was in her early thirties. She was a hard worker, with focus and energy. Brianna was trustworthy. Whenever she says she will do something – you know it will get done. Ade arrived after another couple of minutes. We found a quiet table in the corner so we wouldn't be disturbed. I asked them both what they would like to drink. Ade fancied a pint of beer and Brianna asked for a glass of fresh orange juice so I went up to the bar and bought the drinks as promised, then we were ready to start.

Ade said; *'Since you told us about your experience and the story about looking for miracles and not everyday solutions, I've been intrigued to find out what these Ten Steps are.'*

'Firstly, I need to start by saying that I cannot really explain what happened that night. I was the receiving channel for the Ten Steps. I felt like I was connected to the universe. I truly did. The combination of energy and calmness that I felt was incredible. The steps are simple, and they make good common sense. So, before we start, are you willing to take on board this new experience with an open mind? The reason I emphasise this point is that **in order to change... we must firstly, want to change, to accept help we must genuinely want help**. These Ten Steps will also only work if you are at a certain stage of your life. This stage is usually **when the pain of change is less than the pain of continuing along the path that you're on**. In other words change is the solution So, let me ask you both – are you ready to start?'

Ade and Brianna paused for a moment, looked at each other and said in unison 'Yes, we are ready' 'Great,' I said, 'now let's get started.'

'Ok, what I really need you both to do is to pledge your commitment to me and to yourselves that you are willing to listen, to learn, to apply and then share the Ten Steps with others. Now don't forget, once you start, you must complete all of the steps and exercises. Are you guys ok with that?' I looked them both in the eyes, so they could see that I was being serious. *'Yes, I will make that commitment, Michael. I have seen a changed man in you today and I need to know how you did it so that I can do it for myself,'* said Ade. *'Me too, I absolutely agree with Ade,'* said Brianna.

'I know this may sound a bit over the top, but can you please sign and date this paper here to pledge your commitment? Today, Brianna and Ade, is a special day. As this day will signify the beginning of your path to a fulfilling future. Once you have decided to move forward, make a commitment, and actually have the pledge down on paper for you to see and share with someone else it will increase your commitment to the goal ahead.'

I pledge my commitment to listen, learn, apply, complete the Ten Steps then share the Ten Steps.

_____

Print Name

_____

Signature

_____

Date

Ade and Brianna signed the commitment sheet. Ade said 'I feel like I'm signing my life away,' in a joking manner...

'Well, if you think about it Ade, it is your life we are talking about. We need to take our life seriously, don't we? But thank you for pledging your commitment to the Ten Steps and believing in me. You are a true friend.'

CHAPTER TWO

As Michael starts to share with Ade and Brianna the knowledge that has been given to him from the voice, it has given him newfound inspiration and has reminded him of some of the motivational lessons that he has learned and yet forgotten.

Step One: Accept who you are and where you are today as a beginning and not an end.

'Ade and Brianna, are you ready to start? Well let me begin with Step One.'

'We have all experienced a series of events – circumstances good, bad and indifferent that have brought us to where we are today. **We are the sum total of our environment, experiences, choices and decisions that we have made or didn't make or worse still, even ones that other people have made for us.** That is how we have become who we are today, whether you like it or not.

'Our first step is to accept who we are and where we are today, as a beginning and not fight the past. What has happened, has happened. My mum always used to say; 'There's no point in crying over spilt milk.' It's an age-old saying. Imagine you are lost in the desert. Would you dwell on how you got there or would you focus on how to get out of the desert? Ade and Brianna answered in unison; *'It would be, how do I get out of the desert?'* 'That's right,' I replied

We sometimes spend too much time and energy, focussing on how we got into a mess, rather than how we can get out of it. We look backwards rather than forwards. If you are happy and content with the place you are at today, then it is not a problem. However, on the other hand, if you are unhappy or unfulfilled with the position you are in today and choose to accept it as final, then that is the kiss of death, stress and unhappiness.

'Some people are so caught up in their own problems, telling anyone who will listen that there are no solutions, getting a kick out of the attention and sympathy they receive. This type of person is content to wallow in their own lack of success as an excuse, all the while telling everyone how bad they have got it. The Ten Steps cannot help people like this, they are too negative. The mind is like an umbrella, it only works when it is open. Everybody has an umbrella (a mind), they just need to open it and use it. Especially when it is raining negatives.

'This is why, sometimes, it takes people to be at that point in their life when they are sick and tired of being sick and tired. When they get to this point then they are ready to change. Their minds become open to new suggestions and ideas. The secret is not to wait until you come to this point to take action. Once you have realised that you are unhappy, THAT is the time to take action. Does this make sense?' Ade said; *'Yes, it does make sense. When I look back on my life, I wish that I had taken action sooner rather than wallow in my self-pity.'*

Brianna nodded her head in agreement and said, *'It's just like the umbrella analogy; why wait until you are drenched soaking wet before you put the umbrella up or find temporary shelter? As soon as it starts to drizzle with rain, up goes the umbrella.'* Ade looked at me and then at Brianna, and said, *'Yes, I absolutely get it, what a great analogy, In other words – put your mind into action in a positive optimist way.'*

I took a sip of my drink and popped it down onto the table. I was enjoying the feeling of positivity that was now coursing through my veins. I was happy that I could share the Ten Steps with my friends, and that they were starting to become receptive to what I was saying. I carried on and said, 'Let me ask you another question. **Is where you are today, the slow ending of your life or the beginning of your new life?** I paused and looked them both in the eyes, and carried on. 'You see, it is how you see yourself. Most people don't plan to fail; they just don't have a real plan to succeed. Your current situation can be seen as temporary or permanent. It's your choice. Which one is it going to be?'

'I understand what you are saying,' said Ade, *'But how do you change, when you are stuck in a rut?'*

I smiled at Ade, as I knew that I had the ace up my sleeve and would be able to help him soon with the answer, and I said, 'That is a really good question, and I don't want to look like I am avoiding giving you the answer, but that's what the Ten Steps are all about and I will be going through this with you later. However, if you tell yourself you are stuck in a rut, guess what… **you're stuck in a rut**, and then you have no chance of getting out, have you? You see whatever you keep telling yourself or whatever you keep focusing on becomes your belief and reality.

'Ade, Brianna, listen very carefully to what I'm saying.' They both leaned in towards me, and I had their full attention **'The first step is that you have to accept that if you are in a rut, then use the rut as a beginning and not an end, then work on how to get out of it,** Otherwise, you will be continually stuck in it. Once you accept where you are at today, unconditionally no blame no guilt, that is, your status, your health, your job, your personal relationship, your circumstances, you name it, then you can begin the change. That is where you are today as a new beginning. If you don't accept where you are today as a new beginning, then you are stuck in the past. Is your past, your future…? It only is, if YOU don't change. If you don't change then your past and present is your future.

'You see the words we say to ourselves, that we believe in, control our actions, so we need to be careful what we say about ourselves.

'You are truly a sum total of all your experiences, good and bad. We are the sum total of all the choices and decisions we have made, didn't make or that other people have made for us, negative or positive. There is no one to blame, no guilt, no "I should have known better." That's who you are today and that is your beginning. Accept it When you look at it that way, it doesn't look so bad does it?

'Imagine, Brianna, if you were starting out today. You have your own flat, you're single, you have a decent car, a good job, nice clothes and great friends. A little debt that is all under control as you have said.' Brianna gave a little laugh and replied, *'I don't think that's how I would describe my credit cards. They are definitely not under control.'*

I smiled at Brianna and said 'Well at least you still have your credit cards. If the credit card companies did not see you as a worthy person, they would take them off you or would never offer you them in the first place. You have a social life, your health – which is anyone's greatest asset, and you really enjoy your job. As far as beginning points go, this is a great position to be in. I mean, it beats being ill, homeless, jobless and friendless, doesn't it? Be grateful for what you have today. There is always someone worse off than you. My mum always used to say "Count your blessings, not your messings!"'

Brianna nodded in agreement, then Ade said, 'I see what you mean, it's how you see yourself and seeing where you are today as a beginning. I suppose you could say the same about me. I've got a great partner who I love and is very supportive. We have two lovely children, one is mine and one is from her previous marriage, and I love them both equally, even though they can be a pain sometimes. We have a small house with a small mortgage, but it's ours. I have a job that pays the bills, a car, friends… and as you said, my health and a healthy family.'

It felt good that both Brianna and Ade had taken in what I was saying to them.

'You see, now you are getting into the spirit of it. As a beginning, this is a great starting point, isn't it? I read in a book once by Anthony Robbins "Your past does not equal your future." Every successful person has to start somewhere, and most of them didn't have what you have when they started out. Search the internet or grab a book and listen to or read the autobiographies of some of the most successful and famous people. Most of the stories have the same humble beginnings. **They used their circumstances to empower them, not imprison them.** Our thinking process can empower us or imprison us; it's simply just down to us to see it.'

I saw Matt walking over to the table. He was an acquaintance that we all knew from the pub. He was quite a nice guy but had a tendency to be sarcastic from time to time.

'Anyone fancy a game of pool?' he said enthusiastically.

We all looked at Matt and said simultaneously *'No thanks, We're busy.'* Matt was startled; *'Wow, You guys are intense, what are you so intense about?'*

Ade spoke up; *'Michael has acquired Ten Steps on how to turn your life around, and he has just been explaining it to us, in fact tonight is the first time we've been able to get together for him to explain them to us.'*

Matt cocked his head to one side, looked at us all, and said in a serious tone; *'Can I join in, I've had so much bad luck lately. I need some help.'*

I paused for a moment and said, 'I don't know Matt, this is serious stuff and, there are conditions attached.'

'I am serious," said Matt. 'I'm sick and tired of wasting my life away. Honestly, I'll try anything!'

'Go on, let him join us, we've only just started,' said Ade.

I had my concerns about letting him join us. Matt was larger than life. He was of big stature, had a rugged boyish look with a mop of blond hair, and could be quite outspoken when he wanted to be but eighteen months ago his wife left him. He lost his job and his home and was made bankrupt. This had caused him to become very cynical and sceptical. Life had been very unfair to him. The only thing that appeared to be going well for him was the fact that he was an extremely talented pool player and played for the Rose & Crown team. In fact, when he played pool we saw a different side to Matt. He seemed to come alive; his confidence changed, but at other times he could be very depressing to be with. But, who am I to judge? Everybody deserves a chance if they are serious enough; the Ten Steps are for everyone. I must not forget what the voice said; *'Share the Ten Steps.'*

I turned to Ade and Brianna 'Is it ok with you if Matt joins us?' I asked. 'I don't mind,' said Ade. Then he looked at Matt and said, *'But, Matt, you must promise not to dish out negative comments – you know what you can be like sometimes.'* Then Brianna turned and spoke to him *'Yes I'm happy for you to* join us, but no sarcasm Matt, this is serious stuff and if you are not going to be serious about it, please don't bother.'

'I am serious,' said Matt, 'I've been doing a lot of thinking recently. I need to do something with my life. I just don't know where to begin or what to do. You say that you have these Ten Steps, Michael. Where did you get them from?' 'It's a long story, but first, the conditions of the Ten Steps are that once you have started, you must complete all Ten Steps no matter how you feel about them. It is only with all Ten Steps can you truly reveal the benefits. To only do three to four is like judging a car or a house that is only 30% to 40% finished. It wouldn't be fair would it?' 'No,' Matt replied

'The other condition is that when you have finished the Ten Steps, you must share them with others. One of the greatest satisfactions you will have in your life is helping others. That's what I am doing right now and sharing these Ten Steps with you, so Matt, do you agree to the conditions?' We all looked at Matt; 'Yes, I agree to the conditions, I will take this seriously. You know what I've been like and what I've been through. I need to do something. This is really great for me. I knew I needed help; I just couldn't do it on my own. I feel really good about us all working together as a team.'

'Ok, what I would now like you to do Matt is to pledge your commitment that you are willing to listen, to learn, and to apply and share the Ten Steps. Now don't forget, that once you start, you must complete all the steps and exercises. In other words, you must complete it before you judge it. Are you ok with that?' 'Yes,' Matt replied.

I bent down and got a piece of paper out of my bag. 'Can you please sign and date this paper here to pledge your commitment, because today, Matt, is a special day. As this day will signify the beginning of your path to a fulfilling future.'

Matt signed his pledge of commitment

'Matt, welcome to our group, in fact... we are the first group to do the Ten Steps. Right, let me bring you up to speed. I, like you, have been very unhappy with myself and my circumstances.'

'But I thought you had a great life, in fact, you are one of the few people that I respect' blurted out Matt. *'Thanks!'* said Ade and Brianna with a sarcastic, humorous tone. *'No, sorry, I didn't mean any offence but you know what I mean. Michael always seems to have his act together.'*

At this point I interrupted; 'You know that saying "Never judge a book by its cover?" Well all I can say is that the more I look into the Ten Steps, the more I realise that there are a lot of people just like me, settling for second best or in denial of their circumstances, pretending they are ok, but it's a show. Matt I, myself have been in denial, just like you, I have been unhappy with my life. I'd been searching for answers when on Saturday evening something happened. There was this voice and it was talking to me. I was scared at first but eventually, I just relaxed and listened. I had heard the voice before and ignored it, but this time I decided to listen. I felt like I had been plugged into the universe, then I was given the Ten Steps. The voice told me that there are many people that it has tried to make contact with, but they wouldn't listen. It may have tried to contact you. We all have a little voice that sometimes talks to us which we decide to simply shrug off or dismiss.

'These steps are simple and make a lot of sense, but the voice did say that if the Ten Steps don't work for you, it is because you are not ready to change not because they don't work. Unfortunately, for most of us, we only seem to look for solutions to our problems when we are down or desperate or at a crossroads in our lives. That is when we become more receptive to new information we receive. **It is who you are and how you see yourself and what you do with the information that matters.**'

I paused for breath, took another drink from my glass, and asked my small group if they were ready for me to carry on. In unison, I got a resounding 'YES!'

'Right, you are lucky Matt, we have only just started. STEP ONE is... **Accept who you are and where you are today as your beginning and not your end.** Let me explain to you, Matt. It's all about how you see yourself and your circumstances. Although you are unemployed, broke and divorced, you maintain your own flat, you have some good friends, you're a great pool player, a qualified electrician, and you are alive and healthy. In fact, you are in fantastic shape for a beginner, aren't you?

'When you look at yourself and where you are right now as a beginning, I bet you see yourself differently don't you?'

'I think I understand,' said Matt, slowly.

I could see that he was processing the information that I had just given him, so I then went on to say, 'Let me explain it a bit more. You cannot drive a car safely forward if you are looking backwards can you?'

'No, that would be dangerous,' said Brianna.

'Well, that's the same for us. It would be dangerous, using your words Brianna, to keep looking backwards instead of forwards. Don't get me wrong, **the past is there for us to reflect on and learn from, but we must not live in the past**.

'We need to focus on the present and the future, not the past. What's happened has happened, let it go, let it go. Don't hold on to it, no guilt, no blame, just let it go. **The past teaches us lessons to guide us in the future, the past is not our future.** Let me say that again; **The past teaches us lessons to guide us in the future, the past is not our future.**

'What is safer? Driving constantly looking in the rear-view mirror or looking straight ahead through the windscreen?' Ade and Matt looked at each other with quizzical looks on their faces, as if I was saying something crazy *'Looking through the windscreen, obviously,'* they chorused. 'So, from today onwards, can we all look forward and not backwards?' *'Yes, yes!'* replied everybody.

'You know when you stop and think about it, most of us are brought up to look at our past rather than our future,' said Brianna. *'I feel that, for all these years, I have become imprisoned in my past, I can see that it does make sense. How can we make progress forward, when we keep looking back?'*

'That's right Brianna,' I said, 'and that's what Step One is all about. I think that it is time to do some writing rather than talking, so first we need to make a positive assessment of who we are and what we have achieved so far in our lives.

'Here's something for you all to think about: Does life begin at 1, 10, 15, 30, 40…? **Your life begins at whatever age you decide to begin your life… The decision is yours.'**

Brianna and Ade took notepads and pens out of their bags. *'I haven't got a pen or anything to write my answers down onto,'* said Matt. *'Here you are, have some of mine,'* said Brianna.

They were all sitting poised, pens in hand, waiting for me to talk again.

'Right, what I would like you to do is make a list from a positive approach of who you are. For example; good habits, personality traits, or principles you have that are positive. What do you feel have been your best achievements in life so far? Make a list with as many as you can. How do… *'Slow down Michael!'* said Matt with a smile. *'I can't write that fast!'*

'Ok,' I said. 'I'll give you a few moments.

'Here are a few more examples… What are you good at? What do you own personally that you are proud of? What are you proud of in general? Have you ever wanted something bad enough and got it? Yes? Well, write it down. What makes you happy? What are the positive relationships in your life at the moment and in the past? Becoming a father or a mother? What are your proudest achievements as a child, a teenager or an adult? What gives you your greatest satisfaction in life? Are you beginning to get the picture guys?'

'Yes we are!' they replied

I was on a roll. I felt so full of positivity.

'I have some more examples… what kind of achievements have you made in your life so far? I want you to **make a list of everything that is positive about yourself in your life**. No matter how big or small! What are your best personality traits etc?

'Now, if you find yourself trying to put yourself down – for example, I wasn't really that good at… just ignore it. **This is the old you, fighting the new**

you. Now you've got fifteen minutes; so don't think too much, just write the list. If you're not sure, you can complete this exercise later. I'll tell you what; if you start writing, I will buy you all a drink. No list, no drink!'

Please go to the end of Chapter 2 to complete exercise 1

As I walked towards the bar, I turned around to look at the group. In agreement, they were all writing away. These fifteen minutes gave me time to reflect on the last hour and how well it had gone. I was delighted at how receptive they were to the information that I was giving them. The more I explained, the more I understood myself. Now I understand the power of sharing. The more I give, the more I get.

I ordered our drinks from the barman. 'Same again, please – and whatever Matt usually drinks,' I said.

I just can't explain it, but it was as if I was seeing the world through different eyes. I looked at my watch; fifteen minutes had gone by fast. They were still writing when I went back to the table.

I put the drinks down on the table and said, 'I need to stop you because we still have a lot to go through. This is an exercise that you need to spend quite some time on; I just wanted to get you started so you have an idea of what you have to do in your own time.'

'I have a very busy week ahead; I don't know when I'll find time to finish them off,' said Ade.

'It always amuses me how we can make time to plan a party, a holiday, Christmas, watch a movie, go out for dinner or just to the pub or even go to a football match, but we say that we have no time to plan our lives. It doesn't make sense, does it? I'm sure you can find an hour to invest in your future, it's less time than watching a programme on TV or listening to a CD isn't it?

'We are back to the old saying again, "If you fail to plan, you plan to fail." *'Well I need some help on this,'* Brianna intermitted. *'I feel stupid and even guilty about some of the things that I have written down.'*

23

'I felt the same way too when I first did the exercise, but that's the old you fighting the new you. What did you feel guilty about? I know how you are feeling, but remember we are a team and we all have to support each other. Don't forget that you need to have an open mind and not a judgmental mind. In fact, if we are honest with ourselves, we have all written down things that we probably feel embarrassed about. I know I have.'

'Well, I wrote down that I was a caring person, but I felt guilty because I'm not all the time. There was a time when I didn't care at all,' said Brianna.

'Stop! Stop!' I said, 'No negatives, please. Let's simply analyse this. First of all, nobody and I mean nobody, is perfect. So don't compare yourself to anyone else, because perfection doesn't exist. Even if it did, it is usually temporary. You can be close to perfection. I bet if you asked any top sportsperson if he or she were perfect or could they improve, they would say there was always room for improvement. Let me ask you a question; are you more caring than not caring?

'I suppose I am,' said Brianna.

'Then you are a caring person. We all have admired how, where possible you have gone out of your way to help other people. I would definitely say you were a caring person.' Both Matt and Ade nodded in agreement.

'Isn't it amazing how sometimes we see ourselves in a totally different light to how other people see us? When we receive positive feedback, we need to see ourselves through those eyes and not our negative eyes. It's funny how our brains work. The reason behind this is that sometimes we kid ourselves. If you get an opinion from four or five different people that you respect. They are probably right and you are most likely wrong and need to change your viewpoint and the key is to listen to people that you respect and value their opinions.

'If you want an opinion or answers about furthering your earning potential you must make sure that whoever you are asking must be qualified in the field that you are wanting their opinion on. This, by the way, is only true when the feedback we receive is honest and from a qualified source.

'For example, if you want plumbing advice you would go to a qualified plumber, and not someone who sells cars for a living. Always make sure all the advice you get is from a qualified source, not just because they are a friend or member of your family. Our friends and families are great at giving us advice but most of the time are not qualified in the areas that they are advising us on.

'This is why it is important to accept where you are at today as a beginning. It is also important to build a small team of two to three people that you can use as a reference point to reflect with. These people must be individuals that you respect, trust and that are qualified.'

As I finished speaking, you could hear a pin drop. Ade, Matt and Brianna were sitting there taking in what I was saying to them like sponges absorbing water. It felt great that I was able to impart the Ten Steps onto people who actually wanted to listen and turn their lives around.

'Coming back to my original point,' I said, 'there are parts of you that you like, and there are some parts that you don't like. There are elements that you can change and there are those that you cannot change. To change is difficult, and as a result many people decide to avoid such hard work and remain the same.'

I could see that they were ready for the next step for the evening.

'Right, let's get onto the next step. What I would like you all to do is make a list, for your eyes only, about the parts of you that you feel are negative.; the "bad and the ugly you" if you will. What you don't like about yourself, physically and mentally, your character, bad habits etc. Most people are good at finding fault with themselves and others.

'We do tend to moan and complain about what we dislike about ourselves, for example, I'm too fat, I'm too thin, I don't like my hair, I wish it was straight or curly. My legs are too long. I'm shy and I have no confidence. I'm not good at Mathematics. Now, remember to be honest with yourself. I'm only going to give you ten minutes.'

Ade saw that everyone had finished their drinks. He handed me some money, and said that he would get the next round – but would I mind going to the bar for it?

Please go to the end of Chapter 2 to complete exercise 2a

I ordered the drinks from Femi, the pub landlord.

'What's going on over there?' he asked. *'Oh, we are having a discussion, It's to do with work,'* Ade replied. *'Well if you need any advice, you can come to me,'* Femi said with a wry smile.

As I walked back to the table with the tray of drinks, I was reflecting on what Femi said… It's amazing how everyone in life has an opinion; we just have to be careful whose opinion we listen to…

When I set the drinks down onto the table, I couldn't help but notice that the body language of the group had changed from one of excitement to one of a more sombre tone. Matt appeared to have reverted to his usual default state of depression.

'What's up? You all look really down and depressed.'

'I didn't realise that I had so many bad points,' said Matt.

'I know what you mean,' said Ade in a quiet voice.

I paused for a moment and took a deep breath before I spoke 'Can you see what's happened? That's what happens when you focus on the ugly or the bad you. When you actually analyse these negative aspects later, you will become aware that, actually, it's a negative opinion of yourself that you have bought into. I do apologise for being so harsh, in fact let me give you an example. I've seen a tall man wish he was shorter and a short man wish he was taller. Just stop and think about this, the body that you have got is the body that you have got, all the thinking and worrying in the world is not going to make you taller or shorter, so accept it. Learn to live with it and make the most of it. Look at the actor; Danny DeVito, it hasn't stopped him. Now if you are overweight, you can lose weight. That's something you can change. That's what Step One is all about.

'Now quickly look back at your list and put a tick by the things that you can change, a cross by the ones that you accept you cannot change and a question mark by the ones that you are not sure about. We are going to do this quickly, but you need to do this exercise again and again until you are absolutely sure that you have got the ticks and crosses in the right places.

'Before you start your list; let me tell you a short story I heard about a man that arrived at work one day when he was going to be made redundant and that his employer was unable to guarantee that he would be able to pay him. Knowing his financial situation and how tight his budget was, he became very negative. He phoned his wife to tell her, she, realising how down he was, said; "… Never mind! You know that lottery ticket I bought at the weekend, well, I've won £30,000! So enjoy your day at work and I will see you tonight."

'Now what do you think happened to his state of mind? He went from being negative to a very excited and happy man.' Ade said, *'How long did it take him to change his mental state?'* *'Seconds,'* said Brianna. 'Even if we are negative, we can change our state of mind in seconds if we have a good enough reason to change. Now what type of day would the rest of his day be like?'

'A happy one I should imagine,' said Matt. 'Now imagine he went looking for work straight away, what type of image would he be portraying?' *'A positive and confident one,'* said Brianna. 'Imagine a situation that when he got home, his wife said to him that she will receive the cheque in ten days, but they would not be able to cash the money until he had found a new job. How soon would he be able to find new employment?' *'Days I should imagine,'* said Matt. 'So what you are saying then Michael… **if the reason and motivation is big enough**, you can find a new job in days? That is what the Ten Steps are all about. **They allow us to find what we want and the reasons to go out there and do what we need to do, to get it!'**

'Now imagine after those ten days have passed; the man had got a better job, he had been in a great mood all week and his wife finally told him, "There's no cheque. You sounded so depressed I just made it up on the spur of the moment to try to cheer you up and look, it worked!"

'Oh you're joking,' said Matt. 'I'd shout at her, so would everybody.'

'What would be his state of mind?'

'Negative,' said Matt. 'I would be depressed.'

'That's right, but think about it; has he lost anything?' Everybody paused for a moment … 'No,' said everybody.

'Did he gain anything?'

'Yes,' said Matt, 'He found a new job and was happy for ten days.'

'We can change our state of mind based on false or positive information. This reminds me of the saying; **"Life is 10% what happens and 90% how we respond to it."** A redundancy can be a blessing in disguise. You can use a negative force in your life to change direction and do something more positive, or you can use it as an excuse.'

'I feel that I have been walking around in the dark for the last eighteen months, in fact you're right, I have been using what has happened to me in the past as an excuse,' said Matt,

'Okay you've got two minutes; what I want you to do again is to put a tick by the things that you can change, a cross by the ones that you believe you cannot change and a question mark by the ones that you are not sure about.'

Please go to the end of Chapter 2 to complete exercise 2b

'Do not forget the story I've just told you because there are things that we assume we cannot change, but in fact we actually can change.'

The pub was getting louder; I looked at my watch, it was 10.30 pm and we had been in the pub for three and half hours. I needed to finish off. 'Right your two minutes is up, everyone finished?' '*Yes,*' they all said together.

The next thing I would like you to do is look at the exercise you've done and make a list of the things you don't like about yourself that **you can change**. Affirmation must be written in a positive, present tense as if it has already been achieved.

Please go to the end of Chapter 2 to complete exercise 3

'The last exercise I'd like you to do before we finish off, is to take all the items on your list that you believe you can't change and write the following affirmation, for example, if you are bald, your affirmation will be:

§   I accept my baldness as being part of the unique one and only me and that's why
I'm special and I approve of myself.

§   My baldness is an asset

'Please bear in mind that we will be doing an exercise later on how to construct a plan of action for the things we can change. But this exercise is designed for you to help you accept who you are and where you are at today. Right, you've got five minutes.'

Please go to the end of Chapter 2 to complete exercise 4

Matt was the last to finish, '*I feel so much better now that I have done those affirmations, but I haven't completed all of them,*' he said. '*In fact Michael, I feel a totally different person to the one who came to this pub tonight.*'

Matt had a huge smile on his face. I felt so pleased that I had helped to put that smile there by sharing what I had learned from the voice.

'The key is repeating those positive affirmations over and over and over again until it becomes a part of you.'

Just then, Raj came along and said, *'Matt, do you want to play in the last pool game tonight?'* *'No thanks Raj, I'm busy,'* said Matt. We all looked at Matt in amazement; I've never seen him turn down a game of pool before. 'Matt can I use you as an example to demonstrate something to finish off tonight?'

'Erm, only if it's positive'

'Well I think it is!' I said as I began; 'Matt you are special, there's only one of you and you have some unique qualities. How does that make you feel?' *'Well I feel a little bit special after our exercises today'* 'Okay Matt, you are still holding back a little, but you are beginning to change and this is great. You just need to focus on those special qualities and develop a plan to change the parts that you don't like. That is what our next step is about.

'Matt, how old are you?'

'I'm thirty-three,' he said.

'Well they say that the average person will now live to be over eighty-plus years old in the Western world. If you stop and think about it, that's forty-seven or more years to go. You're not even at the halfway mark. You can all do this same exercise for yourself, just deduct your age from eighty and you will know how long you have left.'

EIGHTY – YOUR AGE = POTENTIAL N° OF YEARS LEFT IN YOUR LIFE

Brianna said; *'It's exciting when you think of your life that way, and you look at how many more years of your life you've got'*

'Exactly!' I exclaimed. 'Now isn't it worth investing the time now to work hard towards your goals, so you can make the next forty-plus years first class, rather than to use your first thirty-three years as an excuse to explain why you never did anything with the rest of your life? Now, Matt, it is not that the first thirty-three years were bad' *'No,'* said Matt, *'it's only a few of those years that were bad.'* 'So why write the rest of your life off, because of a few bad years? That's like having a four-bedroom house and one of the rooms needs redecorating as it's been neglected, so you decide to move out or knock the house down. It doesn't make sense, does it?

'Don't get me wrong, I'm not saying this is easy, but our lives are like a work of art or a sculpture that will never be finished. There is a great deal of hard work to do, but whether you have five, ten, thirty, or fifty more years to go, isn't it worth investing the time now, to achieve as much as you can with the time you have left. **"Learn from the past, but don't live in the past."'** *I've never looked at it that way,'* said Ade. Then he added with a laugh *'I've got at least forty years to go, and I'm going to have some fun and make a difference.'*

This was going really well, so far. Everyone was grasping what I was telling them, and they all appeared to be enlightened by my words of wisdom or should I say the words of wisdom from the voice... I can't believe that I, Michael, would even be saying that! If you had told me just a week ago that I would be talking to a group of people about positivity and making the most of their lives, I wouldn't have believed it. My newfound confidence was thanks to the voice that I decided to listen to.

'So folks,' I said, 'that's Step One; accept who you are and where you are today as a beginning. You are special and unique; **you do not have to get approval from anyone, just yourself**. This is very important. You do not need to get approval from anyone just YOURSELF. There is to be no blame, no guilt, no living in the past and pondering if only I knew better. Isn't that a stupid saying! 'If only I knew better, I wouldn't have done what I did.' If you stop and think about it, if you did know better, you would not have done it in the first place. So, why blame yourself for something you didn't know about in the first place. Moreover, we should see such an occurrence as an opportunity to learn a valuable lesson. It makes far more sense and you feel better. Folks It's time to look to the future. **The future, your future, is as bright as you want it to be, this is your beginning to the new you.'**

'I hope that you all understand that step one is designed to **stimulate** your thought **process**. I heard a saying once, by Earl Nightingale. He said; **"You are what you think about or what you think... you are."** You see; Your thoughts become words. Your words become actions. Your actions become habits. Your habits, become character and your character becomes your destiny. So **if you don't control your thoughts, you don't control your destiny**.

'You need to go through the exercises again and again. I know that I am repeating myself, but this step is about coming to terms with who you are and where you are today as a new beginning.

'I hope that I have helped in some way to partially explain that where you are **today is a beginning**. If we have achieved that today, then we have a beginning… exciting, isn't it?'

Ade spoke, *'I think, speaking for everyone, this has been one of my most constructive evenings I have ever had and I would like to thank you for allowing us to join you.'*

Both Brianna and Matt nodded in agreement. *'Yes, I agree,' they said, almost at the same time*

'Well I am glad that you enjoyed it, the voice did say to share the steps and now I know why. It gives you a greater understanding and a greater sense of satisfaction. Now you are sharing how I feel. For our next meeting, it is probably a good idea if we meet somewhere quieter. Plus I think that I will need a bank loan by the end of the tenth step to cover the drinks bill.'

Ade piped up, *'I've got a great idea, why don't we take it in turns and meet up every night at each other's houses?'* 'That's a good idea, you can come around to mine tomorrow, I will make some snacks,' I said. 'Does everybody else agree?' *'Yes,'* said Ade and Brianna. Matt shuffled in his seat and said, *'I'm not happy about anyone coming around to my crummy council flat, it's not in the best of shape.'* 'There you go again Matt, don't put yourself down, we are all in this together and we accept you as you are today, don't we guys?' *'Yes,'* replied everyone. I stood up from the table and spoke: 'We are a team now.

'Don't forget to do your exercises and please make sure that we keep the Ten Steps to ourselves for now. When you have done all the steps; you can form your own individual groups if you want and tell as many people as possible, okay?' Everybody nodded with collective approval.

We all said our goodbyes and left in good spirits. As I drove home, I was left mentally exhausted, yet I felt a relaxed feeling of contentment and that I was at peace with myself. I was doing something good. 'Thank you, thank you for touching my life' I said out loud in the car in a humble tone, hoping that the voice could hear me.

CHAPTER THREE

Step Two: What is life all about and What is my purpose in life?

The next day in the office was different. Brianna and Ade were still excited about last night. Ade came over to me and told me that when he got home last night, he had spoken with his wife, Lian, had gone through Step One with her and she asked him if she could also join the group. As we were at the beginning of our journey to the Ten Steps, I was more than happy to welcome her into the group.

What a great thing to do as a couple. I hope Isabella and I will be able to go through the Ten Steps together…

Just then Tom came over and started to make some really sarcastic remarks about our meeting yesterday. I stood up from my desk and looked at Tom. I said to him, 'It's easy to make fun of us, but we have much more important things to think about and deal with.'

'Like what?' asked Tom.

I carried on with what I was saying. **'Our lives and our future**. We are at the start of a new beginning and you know what Tom, you've missed out.' I moved from behind my desk and started to walk away. I didn't want any confrontation, so decided to go to the office kitchen to make a coffee. As I walked away, I couldn't help but think to myself – why; when you are trying to do something that is new, good, explorative, or simply trying to improve yourself, that there are always people around you who are negative or sarcastic and are trying to put you down or discourage you.

Why?

Maybe it's because they are insecure and the only way they can hide their insecurity or lack of confidence is to make fun of you and ridicule you. They don't want anything to change, they want everyone to be like them or they will look like the foolish ones.

As I sipped my coffee, Brianna walked in. I mentioned that Ade's wife wanted to join our group, Brianna said that she thought it was a great idea. I took my mobile phone out of my pocket and I sent Matt a message to see how he was feeling. I also mentioned that we had another member of the group and he messaged back saying that it would be really positive for Ade to have his wife on board.

I rushed home from work to get things ready for tonight. I felt a little tense, so I decided to pour myself a glass of red wine from the open bottle that I'd started the other evening. I was wondering how everyone was going to respond to Step Two. The first step had gone well, but this was the most controversial topic of all time. **'What is life all about, what is my purpose in life?'**

This has been a difficult topic since the beginning of time. We can only begin to understand what life is all about and our purpose, when we start to explore, examine it and question life's existence. Sometimes the more you explore, the more disillusioned you get... but we must not give up...

As I sat there with my wine glass in my hand, pondering on the next step, there were so many different opinions. I myself have one, or should I say my latest opinion. What was the real answer? I know the answer I got that evening when I was given the steps, but I still couldn't believe it was that simple. It's amazing – the voice had given me clear direction, but it was still up to me to decide. Just then there was a knock on the door. I had lost all sense of the time and hadn't prepared anything. I quickly organised myself and opened the door.

Ade and Lian were standing at the front door. They both had smiles on their faces. 'Hi guys, I'm sorry, but I haven't prepared anything yet, I lost track of time.' Lian said, *'Don't worry, we'll sort something out...'* They helped rearrange the sitting room to accommodate everyone. The doorbell chimed, it was Brianna and Matt.

I introduced Lian to Matt and Brianna. I noticed there was a relaxed and positive feeling with everybody as they all sat down and started chatting. We were becoming a team. I was wondering what I was going to do for food and snacks. I hadn't had time to eat, so I had a look in the kitchen drawer and found a takeaway menu for the local pizza place.

I asked if everyone fancied some pizza, and they all said that they would.

After a bit of deliberation, we finally decided to get a vegetarian with jalapenos and olives, and a ham and pineapple. I ordered straight away before anyone could change their mind. The pizza company said that it would be around forty minutes to get the order to us as they were very busy.

It was time to start, so we all sat down in the living room with some pens and pads.

'Before we go into the next step, I hope you all did your exercises! It's critically important that you do them as we go along and it's also important that you constantly review them, because as you begin to change, your perception changes too and you see things differently. Keep your exercises up to date as possible with your current thinking. I went through mine last night and I've changed some viewpoints already.'

Matt interrupted, *'I have to say I am really having a problem of accepting what's happened to me and letting go of the past, my divorce, being made bankrupt, not being able to give my daughter things, I feel like a loser.'*

'Now stop right there' I said, 'Where did you get the word loser from?'

'It's how I feel,' said Matt. *'Look at me... I'm a failure'*

Matt's head went down; he went into that depressed mode again. Ade spoke softly and said to Matt *'You can't keep doing this to yourself. Stop beating yourself up mentally. Remember one of the points we made yesterday. **Just because you've had a few lousy years, doesn't mean you are going to have a lousy life.** However, you will if you don't change your views. You are thirty-three years old; remember you've got forty-seven years to go at least.*

Don't judge yourself on the first thirty-three years; you are not even over the halfway point.'

'Matt' I said, 'have you ever watched a football match and by half time your team was down on goals and in the second half, they came out with a different mental attitude and won!'

'Yes I have, so what changed?'

'The manager gave them a good talking to. That's what the Ten Steps are about, giving us a good talking to at half time.

'What he did was focus them on the second half, and remind them about their true potential. The first half was not a true reflection of who they really are. **This is our game, this is our team and this is our destiny.** The second half is ours; we're going to win! Matt, we are going to win aren't we?'

'Yes Michael. It is just so difficult letting go,' he said.

'Can you see why the first step is so important because until we let go, we cannot go forward? **Letting go doesn't mean forgetting, it simply means coming to terms with whatever happened and using that as a positive reference point to grow and go forward.** Also Matt, by whose definition are you a loser or a failure?

'Don't let someone else's negative opinion become your reality. Why does everything have to be judged in a negative way? You have learned some valuable lessons that will help you be a better person, so use it.

'The second step is a question that we all need to answer or try to answer, but most of all you must be happy with your decision. This is going to be more of an open discussion and I need everyone to concentrate, because your answer to this question will determine how you see yourself and your role in life.'

I paused to let everyone settle, then I said to the group 'Are you ready?'

'Yes,' they choroused.

'The second step is… what is life all about? Or should I say what is your life all about? What is your purpose in life? What are your passions in life?' I looked at the faces before me and they all had a startled look. 'Yes,' I said, 'What is life all about? You see your answer to that question **will determine how you live your life and the decisions you make**. In fact, what most of us do is pretend the question doesn't exist and give in to the ways of today. That is: going with the flow, getting a job, getting married, buying a home, having kids, going shopping etc. Enjoying living your life where possible and hopefully dying at a very old age — is that what life is all about? **What is your purpose in life? What mark are you going to leave behind when you die that will say; you were here. What is the legacy you want to leave behind?**

'People of different faiths have their beliefs, atheists have theirs, and scientists have theirs and so and so on. What is yours? In fact, you could ask the question; are your current beliefs your beliefs, or one(s) you adopted from someone else…?' There was a pause for a few seconds; I could tell they weren't expecting this question.

Brianna was the first to speak. *I've asked myself this question several times over the years and then I get distracted by the demands of modern-day living. So I never get to the bottom of it. Well, I can say it's a great question.'*

'All the voice gave me were some clear guidelines but the final decision was ours. It said that the choice is ours to make. We have all been blessed with the gift of choice. One of our great challenges in life is "choice". We can choose to "believe" or "not to believe". We can choose to "act" or "not act". **hat your purpose in life is or what your life is all about, it's your choice. The question is, did you choose your life, your beliefs etc or did someone else choose them for you…A great question isn't it?**

'Now I'm hoping that by the time we finish Step Two, we will all have a clearer idea of what our lives are all about or what direction you want to head in and your purpose in life.

'What's your purpose in life? Another guideline to help you find your purpose in life is before you answer the question; you need to look at the following:

'What are you really good at? We are all born into this world with one or more major gifts. Some people know from an early age, some don't find out until they're older and sadly some people never find out because they are not looking for it.

'So what do you think your one or more major gifts are?

'It's not only the sports people, actors, actresses etc. that have gifts, everyone has. Some gifts will make you a fortune, some gifts will make you appreciated and respected, some gifts will give you peace of mind, self-fulfilment, connection to the universe, some gifts will make you cry and be humbled, every one of us has talents and abilities. Gifts we were born with, blessings and we should know what they are or if we don't, we should look for them.

'So what do you enjoy doing, what would you do every day, even if you didn't get paid to do it? What excites you? What are you passionate about? What gives you your greatest satisfaction when you do it? What do you love to do?

'The answers to these questions give you a guideline to your gifts in life, or your areas of expertise to focus on. Would any of you here, like to share what they are really good at?'

Lian was the first to speak. She looked over at her husband *'Ade is very good with children and coaching them for football on the weekends. He has so much patience.'*

'Isn't it amazing how other people sometimes can see our gifts or areas of speciality clearer than we can? Ade, would you agree with what Lian said?'

'Well, Yes, I suppose so,' said Ade.

'You see that's another problem we have. When we are good at something, we don't acknowledge it to ourselves; we generally put ourselves down by saying I'm not really that good. There is being humble, but we don't need to put ourselves down. If you keep saying, I'm not really that good then you'll never really be that good at anything and never excel at that area. When anyone is complimenting you on your ability, skill or a job done, instead of saying, I'm not really that good, you should humbly acknowledge it and say thank you. You see, Ade, if you are good at training children, and you have the patience, then the question is how can you use this skill to build a career or business? How can you use this skill in other areas of your life? It just needs exploring. Do you get a general idea?' Everyone nodded 'yes' in agreement. 'If you don't feel that you are good at anything when you wake up in the morning, you feel mediocre. We need to feel good about ourselves and that's what the Ten Steps are doing, give us direction and control so we can be more fulfilled in our lives.

'So let's just do a short exercise and try to find out the areas in our lives that we are great at? In fact, you would have answered some of these in the last exercise. Remember the question; What gives you your greatest satisfaction?

'Make a list of the things you would do, even if you didn't get paid for it. What have people told you that you are good at? Write that down.

'What skills in life do you have? What are your areas of specialty, what do you love to do etc?'

I decided to leave them alone for a few minutes to think about what I had said, and to make a list. I stood up and asked if anyone would like a cup of tea or coffee.

I went into the kitchen and made the drinks. I put milk into a jug, took the sugar basin, and popped them all onto a tray to carry through into the lounge. Everyone likes their drinks in a different way. I thought to myself how interesting it was that we all have our own different and special ways, yet some of us don't know what we are special at. Hmmm, food for thought.

Go to Exercise 5

As I made the tea, I couldn't help but think about myself. I was great at organising other people and following a project to completion. I just wasn't good at organising myself. Maybe that is what I need to focus on? Being a project manager...

As I carried the tray back into the lounge, the first thing I noticed was everyone's body language. They were all writing with great energy – except for Matt. 'How are you doing?' I said to everyone. *'Great,'* they replied. Except for Matt. He had his head bowed, looking at a blank piece of paper. *'I'm no good at anything,'* he said in a barely audible whisper.

'How can you say that, you have told me several times that you're a very good electrician. You are also an excellent pool player and you have a heart of gold as you will do anything to help anyone out. You just have to focus on the good parts of you. Matt, come on… what do you love to do?' Matt shifted in his seat and looked up at me. I could see that he felt uneasy about speaking in a positive light when it came to talking about himself.

'Well, to be honest, I love helping people.'

'Maybe that is your area of specialty then. Have you thought about being a care manager, teaching or anything to do with looking after people? This is what we mean by finding out your purpose in life, your passion in life, otherwise you are just drifting. It's sad when you hear someone say, I'm just working to pay the bills, I hate my job. And I think, if you hate it, why do it? Why not get something more fulfilling, go back to college, learn a new trade or career etc.

'You see the more you understand what your life is about and your purpose in life and you look for work or a career that is in harmony with it, you will live a more fulfilled life. Some people from an early age have just known what they want to do, but most don't. Can you see we are all very special in our own different ways? Can you see that?'

'Yes,' they all replied.

'Well,' said Matt, *'I'm afraid I'm one of those people in society who used to believe that life was get a job, get married, buy a house, enjoy life with your family and live to an old age. That is until I got divorced and lost everything. In fact I feel that I have been sent here to suffer, maybe it's because I don't bother going to church anymore.'*

41

'*Don't be absurd,*' said Brianna. '*You are just putting yourself down, just because you don't know the answer. It doesn't mean you have to blame yourself. Going to Church alone won't save you. There are many good and kind people who don't go to Church.* **It's what's in your heart and your beliefs that truly matters.**'

'Sometimes we stop going to church because the church you go to doesn't inspire you, instead of looking around and finding one that does…

'*That's a great point Michael,*' said Ade.

'Church is a place for you to renew your faith, for fellowship to help keep you on the right path, to inspire you to be a good person, to help you deal with life's problems and so on. It's a place for prayer, but going to church alone won't save you… It's going to take more than two hours of worship a week to save you don't you think?'

Lian spoke up and said; '*I was brought up to be a good wife and mother and to serve the Lord, my husband and my kids. To be a good caring person but…*' then she paused, '*I seem to feel guilty most of the time, because…*' and she paused again, Lian had an embarrassed look on her face, '*…because I feel that whatever I do never seems to be enough and that I can do better. When I don't put myself out for my family and friends, I get this guilty feeling. I can hear this negative voice in my head and then I feel even worse, like I have let my family and friends down, I've let God down, it's a horrible feeling*'…

There was complete silence in the room, all you could hear was the wall clock ticking.

'*That's how I feel sometimes,*' said Brianna.

'*It must be a female thing,*' said Matt without thinking about the words that he let tumble out of his mouth. Everyone glared at Matt for not being tactful.

'*I'm sorry, I didn't mean to be disrespectful,*' he said.

Ade put his arm around Lian and gave her a hug. '*I never knew that you felt this way and you put yourself through all that pain. You are a fantastic mother and a fantastic wife.'*

'Lian, Lian,' I said. She lifted her head and looked at me. 'Thank you for sharing that with us. Can I ask you, where did you get that opinion or concept of who you are or who you should be from?'

'Well it was how I was brought up, I suppose. I got it from my parents and from church as a kid.'

'Where did your parents get them from?'

'It's been handed down over time I guess, hasn't it?'

'You see we have opinions and concepts about ourselves but **dare we question the origins of our beliefs and concepts we have of ourselves today?** Dare we? Well, that's what we are doing in this session now. What is life all about? Or should I should say what is YOUR life all about? What's your purpose in life?'

Ade turned to Lian; *'I've never said this to you before, because of your Christian beliefs, but I read this book a few years ago about reincarnation. I can't remember it fully but what stuck in my mind is that we are reincarnated into a family group that allows us to work through our personalities and spiritual souls and eventually you evolve through several reincarnations to a higher spirit. Every now and then I get these déjà vu feelings and I think I've been here before, then I think about my soul being reincarnated, I just can't explain it!'*

'That's rubbish,' Matt said standing up, *'When you are dead, you are dead.'* Matt looked very upset by what Ade was saying.

'Calm down. Let's get back to basics, this is an open discussion, it is not for us to condone or criticise others. Everybody is entitled to their own opinion, whether you agree or not, we must, as a group, respect them.' Matt sat back down and apologised for his little outburst.

'You see there are really so many opinions, concepts and beliefs about religion. Whatever else you want to call them, about what life is all about and these opinions and beliefs control us directly or indirectly. For example, some people say that because there isn't a God, we can do whatever we want because we don't have to answer to anyone else except ourselves… Some say because there is a God, we have to be careful what we do and think, because we have to answer to God… Others say I did believe in God but since I lost my mother, my job or since that disaster, there can't be one. The list goes on.

'There are so many religions, churches, institutions, non-believer institutions, etc, that it can be hard to choose which one and it can be confusing, so we do nothing!… As I said earlier, sometimes you could just be going to the wrong church.

'Is life about paying your bills, your mortgage, credit cards, clothing, playing golf, eating out, football, watching TV etc. Is that it? Is it caring for others, sacrificing yourself, putting everyone first before you, getting married, kids, divorce etc.? What is life all about?'…

Just then the doorbell went; it was the pizza delivery man. 'Good timing,' I said, 'Time for a break.' We all had a cup of tea, some pizza and discussed each other's beliefs and opinions. *'Well, Michael,'* Ade said, *'Are you going to tell us what life is all about?'* Everyone settled back down.

I leaned forward, 'First let me say that there are institutions that have their beliefs on the real answer and we are not here today to knock or disbelief any of them. What we must all agree on is, there must be a purpose to life and it isn't just about getting a big house, a promotion, being a good parent etc. That's part of it, don't get me wrong there is nothing wrong with advancing and being at the top in whatever field you're in, so long as your achievements have been done honestly and ethically. You can be a nurse, a carer, a doctor, work in the services, caring and help people in the community. This could be your vocation in life; it doesn't matter so long as you are happy and fulfilled.

'Now! Some people's beliefs are that too much money is not good for you and money makes you a bad person. Wrong! Money is like alcohol to some people, it brings out the fun, creative, good person and to others, it brings out the worst in them. It is the idolisation of money that is bad for you.

'**We are all born successful** and one of our goals in life is to develop ourselves to the point where we have more than enough for ourselves. So we can share with others the extra surpluses we may have, be it money, material things, spiritual, time or just plain love and caring. The challenge is when we get too selfish.

'There is an old song, I think Diana Ross sang it; "Reach out and touch someone else, help the world to be a better place." "Imagine" by John Lennon. Imagine we all, I mean we all tried to make the world a better place, what would the world be like? I love that Michael Jackson song, "Man in the Mirror". If you want to change the world, look in the mirror and change that man in the mirror first. Another one of Michael's songs "Heal the World, Make it a Better Place"; there are so many messages out there to receive.'

'What about the Black Eyed Peas song, "Where is the Love?"' said Matt.

'There are so many songs about hope, changing the world making a difference that uplift you. Imagine everyone in the world coming together and working on making the world a better place, wow, just think about what we could achieve. It's a shame we are imagining instead of this being part of our culture.

'I have a question for you: **Will your life contribute to making the world a better place?'**

'Wow, what a question, I have never thought about it,' said Matt.

'Me neither,' said Brianna.

'Will my life contribute to making the world a better place? Wow, great question,' said Ade.

'**It's so easy to exist but it's difficult to exist and persist with purpose.** So what is your purpose?' asked Michael.

'How can societies or businesses function with no managers, no one taking control? Everyone has a role to play in the big game of life; you just have to decide your role in the big game of life. Imagine a giant jigsaw puzzle, every piece has a role to play and if there are a few pieces missing, the jigsaw just doesn't look right and so it is with us. Everybody is special and has a role to play. **The question is; are you playing the right role or the wrong role in your game of life?**

'Remember the Ten Steps are not for everybody, many are content with their lives or happy not looking to change. **The Ten Steps are for those who know within themselves, they are not fulfilled, something is missing, and there is more they have to offer life. There is more they have to give.**

'Let me say this again, the Ten Steps are for those who know within themselves, they are not fulfilled, that something is missing and there is more they have to offer in life and give.

You can only achieve when you are with like-minded people…There are some people – back at the office that this would be a waste of time on – unless they change their views and values

'Can you imagine a business or organisation with no team leaders, supervisors, foremen, managers, and no managing director? Nobody was responsible for the viability of the company. Can you imagine getting a bus, train, and an aeroplane with nobody driving or flying, taking control? What are the chances of success? None! **Having a meaning to your life is like putting the driver back into the bus and the pilot back into the plane.**

'We call ourselves human beings, what is a 'being'? We are the most advanced species on Earth today. Our role has been to evolve but **who is in control of what you are evolving into**? Who is driving your car, who is flying your aeroplane? Who? **Have we accepted the 'automatic pilot' system of evolution that society and the politicians have given us?** Which is becoming more and more predictable, have you?

'The world is becoming smaller and the mysteries of the world are becoming fewer. What's exciting though, is people's awareness is growing, people are searching, looking for solutions, just like us. Is everyone following me so far?'

'You really have us all thinking!' exclaimed Ade with a smile

'I was fortunate to go on a safari in South Africa. It was an amazing life experience, but I remember when we were leaving at the end of our trip, I couldn't help but think – what is life is all about and how similar we, as humans, were with the animals.

'You see life in the jungle was about –
1. Surviving any predators, looking after your family if you have any.
2. Having to find food to eat for you and your family to survive and finally
3. Reproducing.

'It was simple and it didn't matter whether you were a lion, an elephant or a gazelle. On many wildlife programs, the threat to a herd of deer or buffalo is only when the lion, cheetah etc is hungry. Once these predators have eaten, everyone is safe.

'Now, as humans we are more sophisticated, we have cars, houses, clothes etc, but when you stop and think about it, what's the difference?' *'None I suppose,'* said Ade. *'So is that what life is about? Surviving predators, eating and reproducing? Is that it?'* 'Well yes to a certain point,' I said. **'It is those three, and a purpose.** You see most people live their lives to survive predators, looking after their families, eating and reproducing and there's nothing wrong with that, but then there are those of us who believe we can do more, make a difference, change lives, change the world, serve spiritually. There is more to humans than an animal.

'The human being has all the same organs as a lion or a gorilla. We are the only species that if you gave us a piece of land and came back to us in six months' time we would have a home, a fire to cook with, clothes etc and with every other species they would be left with the same land they were originally given.'

'We as humans today are very special, all of us are born with unlimited potential, and that's **our great challenge, realising our potential. Has the world seen the best of you or do you have more to give?**

'They say we only ever use 5–10% of our brainpower. It's just that **between birth and twenty years old, we get conditioned and our confidence is taken away**. Think about it, we are told more about what we can't do instead of what we can. By the time you get to fifteen, eighteen and twenty years old, most of your confidence has been taken out of you. You talk to a five-year-old and ask them what they want to do and they have these great goals and ambitions. Talk to the same person at twenty and it will be a different conversation.'

'Yes,' said Brianna, 'I never thought of it that way, we get conditioned through our parents, education, society, circumstances, success and failures, to accept where we are at as that's our life. So if we are not brought up to search for our potential as a person, what do we do? Ask yourself why don't they bring us up to search for our potential? Because society is designed to control us, not empower us!'

'Well we can achieve through education, can't we?' said Ade.

'Education is great but it still limits us. **This is not a, let's blame things on society, education, families etc, this is just about our awareness.** Qualifications etc. are important, they put you higher up the chain, but is that what this is all about and if you are not academic what then? We are forced to get a job in a factory, office, minimum wage etc. and fight our way through life. Other options are to start a business, get into a sales career etc., if you have the belief and commitment. Sales is one of the few professions where you can have no qualifications, come in, train and work your way to being one of the top earners...

'At conception, there are millions of sperm cells but only one, with its unique DNA, makes it and fertilises the female egg, **creating the one and only you. You are one in millions.**

How does that make you feel?

'There are twenty-three pairs of human chromosomes, twenty-three from your father and twenty-three from your mother. During fertilisation, the twenty-three single chromosomes from each parent, pair off, for example, chromosome number twenty, pairs off with their appropriate "partner chromosome", number twenty. Now the two chromosomes in a pair contain the same basic genes, for example, the colour of your hair, eyes etc. Chromosomes number twenty-three are the only two chromosomes that decide whether you turn out male or female. They are called the X and Y chromosomes because they look like an X and a Y.'

'Is that where the terminology "The X-Factor" comes from?' said Ade in a joking manner.

'I don't know, maybe.' I said. 'But it's a good point, we all have the X factor and the Ten Steps is a simple process to find out what your X or Y factor is and go for it. You see the contestants when they start in the *X-Factor* TV program, have the raw talent and each week they are trained and groomed and by the end of the show you have a star. That's what the Ten Steps will do for you, take your raw talent and guide and shape you into who you want to be, but first, you have to have the courage to simply step up and put yourself forward, you have to believe in yourself. The winner of the X factor would never have won if they didn't take the first step of entering the contest, and sometimes they don't even put themselves forward when somebody else does it for them because they believe in them.

'Please make a note of who believes in you. Why do they believe in you? Please write that down.'

'My mum believes in me,' said Matt.

'Mums are the best, but outside of Mum and Dad who believes in you? Seriously though, this leads to a set of unique individual characteristics from the two sets of chromosomes and that's why we inherit features from both parents, but we still remain a unique individual, with all our own unique DNA.

'You are special! You are a one off. Think about it, there's only one of you on the planet. How does that make you feel?'

'Makes me feel special,' said Ade.

'Me too,' said Brianna.

'There is nobody on earth like you with the same genes, but it's up to us to realise our own potential. Society will not do it for you; you have to do it for yourself. You have to take control and accept the responsibility for your success.

'The next time you look in the mirror, say to yourself, **"I am UNIQUE, I am SPECIAL, I am the ONE and ONLY me. I have a purpose in life and I have a life to live for. I accept 100% responsibility for my life. I asked my god, my higher power, the universe to direct and guide me. I am evolving to be the best me I can be." That's** what the Ten Steps are all about.'

'Gosh, Michael,' Matt said, *'You don't half feel special when you look at yourself that way.'*

'I know,' said everyone else, in agreement.

Brianna jumped in. *'It's very difficult to change the way you think, when you have been brought up that way.'*

'**Change is not easy** at the best of times, but **the only way that you can change is when you are ready for change and understand you need to change**. Sometimes change comes about because we are forced into it, due to a set of circumstances. It is life's way of getting you to re-access your life, your values, your beliefs and your perceptions. I like the saying from Albert Einstein; "In the middle of every difficulty lies opportunity."

'Think about this, when times are difficult, do you look for the opportunity or just focus on the problem?' *'I focus on the problem,'* said Matt. 'Remember what we said at the start, we spend more time planning a birthday party, Christmas, or a holiday than we do planning our lives. When we have a problem, we spend more time on the problem, rather than the solution to the problem.

'Let me give you another viewpoint. Imagine it was your funeral and your friends, family and workmates were going to say a few words about you. What would you want them to say? How would you want to be remembered?

What legacy would you want to leave behind? Some people leave a will behind, that's for your material belongings, what about how you touched other peoples' lives? What would you leave? It doesn't have to be just people like Carnegie, Rockefeller, Edison, Churchill etc., we all contribute. Pardon the comparison but life is like a pizza. Your body, mind and soul are like the dough, but it is up to you what toppings you have on it. Do you want to be a simple cheese and tomato, in fact using this example, if you were a pizza, what pizza would you be? Remember you can be any pizza you want to be and you can change the toppings when you want.'

Matt replied with a grin, *'I'm a thick crust spicy hot one with jalapeno chillies for a topping.'*

'I'm a thin crust ham and pineapple with mushrooms. Quite plain, but with a bit of sweet fruitiness thrown in,' said Brianna with a little giggle.

'We're all different, aren't we? Let me give you another analogy. Imagine a fantastic buffet with all different kinds of foods from all over the world, cooked by the finest chefs. You could go up to the buffet as many times as you want and the buffet is there twenty-four hours a day and 365 days a year. Would you only eat what you knew or would you experiment and try different things?

Ade chimed in with no hesitation, *'I would definitely experiment.'*

'You see life is like a buffet meal; you choose what you like and want but don't be afraid to experiment and try something else. You have to come out of your comfort zone. If you don't like it, you can change it for something else, the choice is yours – **you choose it's your life**. Nothing is permanent, so you can keep changing and trying new things, and hang onto the ones you like that give you the greatest satisfaction.

'The Ten Steps are trying to make you more aware of the life you have chosen consciously or unconsciously and if you don't like the life that you have, these are the simple steps to help change. Now I know I said simple, I didn't say it would be easy and this only applies to those who are looking for a more fulfilled life.

'We live in the most abundant society there has ever been, opportunities galore. There are so many stories and examples of people from all walks of life that have turned their lives around. Why not you? Why not you?... Richard Branson was expelled from school and look at what he has achieved today. Anything is possible so long as we have the **Desire, Determination, Discipline, Belief and Persistence to go after the life we want**.

'There are people in their sixties and seventies going back to university, what admiration I have for them. You see if your life is about serving your country and you do that, you're successful, if it's about being a good wife, father etc you've succeeded. I'm not saying that your life should be about climbing Mount Everest, becoming a millionaire etc. What Step Two is about is to **determine what you want your life to be, not what you have settled for**. Let me say that again, Step Two is about **what you want your life to be and not what you have settled for! Don't settle for second best** It's important to also understand that the fact that you have had a go; you made an attempt to do something with your life is very important and in itself fulfilling.

'**Life is a balance of family, health, career and spiritual goals.** There is no set order, you have to, however, at specific points in your life, change your priorities to focus more and develop that part of your life, be it a career, family, health or spiritual etc. The hardest part of life is getting the right balance because we are forever changing as people, our priorities today are different from five to ten years ago. At sixteen your perceptions of life are totally different to how we are today aren't they? To develop any part of your life you have to put time and commitment in and there lies another challenge in the modern world we live in; **time, yes, time**. We are back to that same point again; it's amazing how we make time to socialise, clean, cook, go to the pictures etc, but no time for sorting out our lives out. It takes till we're forty, fifty or sixty-plus years old before we realise and sometimes it's too late, but it's never too late to change because **life is about evolution**.

'**The key is; are we in control of what we are evolving into?...**

The Earth is a small planet in the galaxy. **We are not the centre of the universe anymore**. The world we lived in then had changed and would never be the same again.

'We need new definitions to explain births, deaths, earthquakes, floods, good harvest etc and thus we created the birth of the modern age. We sent explorers out, scientists, to bring back a complete explanation of our existence. Is there really a God?...

'This was to take time, so we the Western world as a race took faith into our own hands. We focused on ourselves and became preoccupied developing a better and more secure life for our family and ourselves, thus, **the industrial age was born**.

'This was the beginning of the reduction in the gap of the class system. It was not which family you were born into; it was what you did with your life. Henry Ford built the T100 car, making it possible for everyone to own a car. The Western world today lives in an age where we can have up to three or four cars to one home.

'So what happened after the Industrial Age...

'The Information Age was born...

'Computers, mobile phones, androids, texts, Facebook, Instagram, YouTube, Siri, WhatsApp, Telegram, Alexa, Google, not to mention branding, satellites, space travel, etc. you name it, the world information at a touch, total access to the world, exciting, real live time information at your fingertips, everyone's opinion paraded on social media, good, bad, ugly, and that has now evolved to noise, information overload, selective listening, information burnout, you just have to see how many people are on their phones when you go out, social media has taken the brain over no time to think, reflect, reassess, then we had the Covid pandemic, so where do we go from here? **The awareness age! We are seeking meaning and belonging.**

'In all the activity that has gone on in the world, we have forgotten to ask that question, **what is life all about?** Don't get me wrong **we need to work to live, but what about the other things in life that make us feel fulfilled. What are we giving back to the world? What is our contribution to the world? Not what can the world do for us. The pandemic has been a world reset forced on us. A time to reflect, to re-evaluate, what's important,** what's not important, to refocus, to re-energize your values in life, to review your priorities in life... the list goes on, what's your take away? The world has shifted, have you?

'I believe the world is waking up and people are now beginning to seek a more holistic and spiritual approach to life. Will this be a new age?

'Not everyone is capable of looking from this viewpoint, you have to be at that point in your life or you won't get it 100%. Please I am not trying to point a finger at the world and say all we have achieved is wrong. Far from it, **we have created an amazing world.** I'm just pointing out that there are a lot of great things that have been achieved, but we can add to them and enrich the quality of our lives. **We just need to care for each other more and look after the world.** So, now you understand how we have evolved today as a society.

'The world is evolving, you can't stop it... I know I feel like I'm being sucked in and just going with the flow. It's time to stop and take stock of who you are and what you want to do with your life. **Control your evolution...** I'm not talking about success or material wealth, **I'm saying "Be the best you, you can be."** Take back control of your evolution...'

'That's a great question Michael,' said Ade. *'Am I today, the best me I can be?'*

'I love music, do you?'

'Yes,' replied everyone.

'Well I have always found it amazing after hundreds and hundreds of years we can still write a new song about love, moving isn't it? We can improve on anything we want to...

'So, **what is life all about?** The voice explained that it is for you to decide. What I will give you is a guideline to follow... listen carefully; this is how the voice explained it to me. **Life is about taking your circumstances and challenges and using them to evolve yourself into a better and more wholesome you. It is an endless journey of self-improvement, spiritually and** mentally. It's learning how to touch and help others, helping to make the world, your community, a better place. It's learning how to balance your career, family, health, material and spiritual goals. It's about connecting to your higher power. Your God if you believe. Life is about realising how special you are, your purpose and how special everyone is and respecting each other.

'It's about enjoying the nice and simple things in life. The beauty of a daffodil on a spring morning, watching the sun rise or set. Everyone has a role to play in the game of life. Some people are ahead, some are behind. It does not matter and it is not a race. It is your life and it's not anybody's fault, nobody to blame, it's up to you what you do with it. If it is to be, it's up to me! You are born to win. It's about being the best you that you can be.

'Your life is about discovering what life is all about in an honest and ethical way and then living it with passion and doing all this with your faith and belief.

'One of your main purposes in life is to make sure you are evolving into the best you, you can be and there is only one of you in the world. So when you go to your grave, you can say, I was the best me I could be, I was here. Congratulations! I contributed.

'Fear, blame and guilt are some of the best control mechanisms that society uses to control and manipulate us and keep us down. We have a problem; we blame ourselves instead of looking for the cause. Find the cause, then you know exactly what to do. Change the effect into what you want. Seeing it as a challenge, an opportunity to grow from and an opportunity to rise above the problem. **Accept the challenges of life, so that you may feel the excitement and satisfaction of achievement.** Think back in your life when you have accepted a challenge and won, how you felt, you felt fantastic didn't you?'

'Yes,' everybody replied.

'The saddest epitaph is here lies Mr. or Mrs... Who could have been... They never competed in the game of life; they let the pressures of the modern-day hold them back. They never achieved their true potential, because they just went with the flow.

'How many times do we make excuses for our lack of fulfilment? **You see you either have reasons to succeed or excuses to fail**! Whether you like it or not, rich or poor we all have challenges, problems whatever you want to call them, life is about the choices we make or don't make and how we deal with them and how we use them to grow, rather than imprisoning ourselves in problems and self-pity.

'There was a story I once heard. There was a great and wise King who used to hold court for his people one day of every week and anyone from his Kingdom could come and ask questions and get advice.

'The King would try to help everyone with his wisdom. One day a young man thought he would make a fool of the King, so he planned a plot. He would hide a small bird in his hand and ask the King if the bird was dead or alive. If the King says the bird is alive he would squeeze the bird and kill it. If the King says it was dead, he would let it live and fly away. His time came and he went before the King. "Your Majesty," he said, "I have a bird in my hands, is it alive or dead? The king paused, looked at the young man for a moment and said...

'**"Young man it is, as you will it,** the choice is yours."

'**Life is how you see it, it's in our hands;** good or bad, happy or sad. How do you see yours? Are you alive in this world or are you the walking dead?

'I'm not talking to the world; I'm not dealing with world issues; **we're just simply talking about you and me**. How do we see the world and what do we want our lives to be? **So let's keep it simple**, no politics, please!

'It is never too late to start. Sometimes it takes a near life-threatening illness to wake us up or through suffering, a redundancy, a divorce, or our modern day diseases, stress etc. to wake us up and ask the question — what is my life all about? Well here is the answer, are you ready for this? **Your life is about**

discovering what life is all about in an honest and ethical way and living it! Imagine at eighteen going to college and doing a course about what your life is going to be about! Doing a course on goal setting where would we be today? Doing a course on spiritual living.'

'It's not worth thinking about it,' said Brianna.

'I would be a pilot,' said Matt. We all stared at Matt. *'I always wanted to be a pilot, but my dad wanted me to learn a trade, so I became an electrician, then I got married and you all know the rest.'*

'Life is a journey in which we experience the good, the bad and the indifferent. It's how we grow from these experiences that make us better people.

Matt interrupted me and exclaimed, *'Wow, this is some deep stuff. It's getting really heavy isn't it?'*

'Yes, but can't you see we always seem to be avoiding the deeper issues in life and settling for the easy answer. If we're going to look at a picture, let's try and look at the whole picture. Once you can clear your mind, the future is yours.'

Matt thought for a second or two as he mulled over what I had just said, and slowly nodded his head in agreement.

'If you are a Christian and a believer, a Jew, a Muslim or whatever religion you are – and you believe in God, I don't have to explain God to you, but to the non-believer please hear me out.

'First, your definition of God must not be restricted to a super God with rights and wrongs.

If you do not believe in G.O.D, you should believe in G, double O, D; that is G.O.O.D.

'God or Good can be eternal peace and love. Have you ever noticed when you are thinking good thoughts, how at peace you are with yourself?' I looked at everyone as I was saying this. No one answered. They were all very deep in thought.

'The voice then said 'I am not preaching Christianity or any other religions, I am asking you to question your beliefs. Not whether there is a God, a higher power or not, but to question where those beliefs have come from and why? If you believe there is a God, then why? If you don't believe there is a God, then why? Does it have to be scientifically proven? Millions of people believe they can win the lottery, but millions of people don't believe in having faith. Was man created from the Big Bang theory? You have been given a gift of choice. Choose wisely… I'm asking you to look into your heart.

'Here's something else to think about. Earth is suspended in an infinite galaxy. Go to the natural history museum in London and you will find we are a small speck in the big picture. The earth, like us, is dependent on the sun for survival, that's another miracle that happens every day; sunrise and sunset, we take it for granted. Whenever you can, watch the sun set or the sun rise, it's amazing. There has to be a creator, a higher power, a source, a power for Good it is for you to decide what your definition of that is. The question is whether you believe that there is a creator, then what is your definition of your God/creator?

'If you are a non-believer then just believe in G.O.O.D. Be a Good person. That is the foundation of a healthy mind and the beginning of your spiritual journey.

'In each and every one of us there is a good side and a dark side, the choice is yours. It is easier not to believe. You don't have to be an evangelist but understand the choice is truly yours. **It is easier to be bad than good.** We live in a society today that if you are a good person, some people won't like you and if you are a bad person some people respect you. In fact we respect tough people more than nice people. It's quite sad, isn't it?…

'Matt, Ade, Lian and Brianna you need an open mind to establish first that there must be a creator, the question is, **is our creator scientific or spiritual or both, is it a higher power or energy?** The voice said, I will not give you the answer because you have to choose. It's your choice and your decision. Choose wisely. What is your explanation?... Even though we cannot fully explain it, there must be a creator.

'When you look at the human being, how our internal organs work, how effectively everything works keeping you at a constant temperature, healing you, processing food , air etc., let me ask you a question. **Does everything in life have to be explained?** We wake up every day and expect daylight or the sun to shine. We also expect it to go dark at night and this process of day and night to repeat itself forever. The thought of the earth revolving around the sun and the moon. The earth revolves at approximately 1,117 times per minute, how does it do that? A scientist would give you an explanation. Imagine that there was no sun, there would be no light. How long would the world last? So our total existence is based on another body. Who controls the universe? Yes we are special, but are we so daft to think that the world revolves around us.

'It is time for us to make peace with ourselves and figure out what our purpose in life is. This is not a question that can be answered in five minutes but give it time and thought, do your research and in time the answer will come. Remember your purpose today does not mean it is your purpose for the rest of your life, because circumstances change. We are constantly evolving. We need to focus on achieving a balanced life. Don't make paying your bills, budgeting etc more important than a happy family life or vice versa. The challenge is balance; this is not easy and can be very difficult. Remember to bring balance; we must sometimes prioritise certain areas first. I know I am guilty of prioritising work and not bringing the family back into balance.'

'So, in closing this session, **our beliefs control our attitudes in life and how we see life and our attitude controls the actions we do or do not take, and these actions control our happiness and destinies**. It is time for you to decide what your life is all about, what your beliefs about God or a higher power is and how you can implement all this within your everyday life. **You are born to win, but it's up to you what you fight for or stand for, the choice is yours.** I like the saying, if you don't stand for something, you will fall for anything. Add your beliefs to your purpose in life and you have someone who is unstoppable. Yes you are unstoppable!

'Now, guys, I know tonight has been intense'

'Hey Michael, intense is not the word, this is heavy stuff. Boy, my head is spinning, but it does all make sense,' said Brianna.

'Yes, therefore we will not meet tomorrow to allow you to explore and determine your beliefs and the actions you need to implement. I hope I haven't confused anyone, the voice did tell me that this step would be the most challenging one.'

'I have to be honest with you, Michael, but I don't know if I understand or agree with all you have said tonight,' said Ade.

'Well that is why we need tomorrow to ponder on it. Go over everything we have said tonight, do your exercises again and again, until you get it clear in your head. Do some research on your own. Speak with your conscience and make the right decision for you, yes you...'

'Please remember change can be instant, but sometimes the circumstances you are in means that you can't just drop everything and change overnight. We live in an instant world and we want everything now... life doesn't always work like that, it needs time. We see the world through our beliefs and that's why.'

'It's important that you clear things up. There is no who's right or who's wrong. It's how you see it. It's now time to put your brain to work, **just remember you are special, a miracle, you have a purpose**, it could be as simple as bringing up your children with certain values or climbing Mount Everest, or being the top in your field. It is up to you what you want to achieve.'=

'So, in summary, Step Two is about establishing what your life is about, what your purpose in life is? What are your beliefs; GOD, GOOD or Non-believer? This is just a guideline on what life is about. Life is about exploring and discovering what life is about.

'Life is about taking your circumstances and challenges and using them to evolve yourself into a better and more wholesome you. It is an endless

journey of self-improvement spiritually and mentally. It's learning how to help others, helping to make the world, your community, a better place. It's learning how to balance your career, family, health, material and spiritual goals. It's about connecting with your higher power. Life is about realising how special you are and how special everyone else is. It's about smiling every day. The beauty of a daffodil on a spring morning, the sunrise or sunset, a smile on a baby's face. It's about experiences and dealing with love, hate, pain, joy, sadness, happiness etc. Leaving a legacy behind for people to follow…

'It's about enjoying the nice and simple things in life. Everyone has a role to play in the game of life. Some people are ahead, some are behind. It does not matter and it is not a race. It's your life and it's not anybody's fault. Nobody to blame, it's up to you what you do with it. You are born to win. It's about being the best you, you can be. Your life is about discovering what life is all about in an honest and ethical way and living it with passion.

'Step Two is about establishing what you want your life to be, not what you have settled for.'

'It's now time for you to use the arguments put forward and make your own mind up on what's your life all about and what your purpose in life is! So this is your exercise to do at home.

'There is a meditation process I would like you to do first before you start and write any answers down. Meditation is the practice of thinking deeply or focusing your mind for a period of time. You can do this in silence, or with the help of music and guidance. There are some great meditation guides on YouTube.'

EXERCISE 6: Chapter Three, second Step: What are my beliefs? Do I believe in God?
>   **What is my life about?**
>   **What is my purpose in the next year, three years and five years?**

'Thank you all for coming tonight. As I said, take tomorrow off, this is too serious a topic not to give it time, look over the notes and please do the exercises.'

Ade said that we should have the next meeting at their home. Brianna and I had been there several times but Matt hadn't, so Ade gave his address and mobile number to Matt and he put them into his phone.

Lian looked at the time on her phone. *'Oh, wow, It's after midnight. I can't believe where the time has gone. We must get back home as the babysitter will be wondering where we've got to.'*

'Those new beliefs you have are for your eyes only. Only you need to know what your life is all about, look for the positives within. So, goodnight everyone and thanks for listening.'

We all said our goodbyes and I did a quick tidy up.

I sat in my favourite armchair and reflected on how well the evening had gone. I was mentally exhausted but had a wonderful feeling of accomplishment. Everyone was right – This was a heavy subject, but it also was a very important one.

I wanted to unwind a little before I went up to bed, so I made another cup of tea, stirred in a spoonful of sugar, and put on one of the ten-minute meditations that I had recently found. I closed my eyes, and listened to the relaxing deep tones of the meditator's voice as it told me how to breathe and clear my thoughts…

CHAPTER FOUR

Step 3: Determine what your goals in life are!

Wednesday flew by in a bit of a blur when I was at work. Ade and Brianna tried to discuss Step Two with me, and I sort of avoided their questions. As I said to them, there is no right and wrong, but it is amazing how unconsciously we subscribe to a thought, an idea or opinion, but we are not conscious of when we made that commitment to that thought, idea or opinion.

All Step Two is about is for us to consciously make our own decisions of what our lives are about, knowing we also have the right to change our opinions at a later date if we wished to do so.

Most people just settle for the lives they have got. While some go after the lives they want. That is what the Ten Steps are all about, for the few of us that believe we have more to give life. Life is learning how to balance your career, family, health, material and spiritual goals. It's about enjoying every day. It is an endless journey of self-improvement. Life is simply about taking our circumstances and challenges and using them to evolve into a better and more wholesome person. I couldn't help but think how I had messed my life up and used my circumstances and challenges as an excuse to imprison myself, rather than use it to develop me and empower me.

It was time to go home; I needed the night off to start tidying up for when Isabella and the kids came home. I was missing them, but at the same time, I was dreading Isabella's reaction to the Ten Steps. It had been a while since I had been on my own. Gosh, the housework, what a chore, what a mundane and thankless job. I needed to appreciate Isabella more for all the little things she does. In fact, I needed to plan and organise in advance for Isabella's arrival. We spoke every day on the phone, I had only told her little snippets of the Ten Steps, she had responded negatively to what I had to say, so I knew I had a big job explaining them to her when she got back.

I rushed home, had my dinner and cleaned up, did the washing, vacuuming etc. I was going to be ready for Isabella. The hardest people to convince are those that are close to you. I was shattered, so I had an early night.

Thursday at the office was a nightmare, the computers had gone down and when we got them back up, we had lost three days' worth of data. It was my job to do the backup and I hadn't done it, not the extra pressure I needed at the time. However, I survived the day and was looking forward to tonight. I was very glad to leave the office; Tom had been making sarcastic jokes again. Why is it there are always people around trying to put you down when life is tough enough as it is? No wonder why so many of us fail to aspire to anything, **we can't handle the criticism and persecution.** Well, I am not going to let Tom or anyone get the better of me, this is my life and now with the Ten Steps, I have the keys to open the doors I want to.

I went to the gent's bathroom, looked at myself in the mirror and told myself – I am unstoppable! I am unstoppable! Wow that feels good. It's amazing how you see yourself, when you look at yourself and circumstances from a positive perspective and not a negative one.

When I got home, I had a quick shower, something to eat and quickly reviewed Step Three for tonight. This was going to be fun and interesting to see everyone's reaction, especially after Step Two.

We all seemed to arrive at the same time at Ade and Lian's. Lian made us all a drink and we chatted with each other. Everyone seemed to be in high spirits. Everyone except Matt.

I asked Matt if he was alright. He looked a little down, but he said that he felt ok. I didn't believe him, but I wasn't going to push him. If he wanted to tell me, he would in time.

I simply said to him, 'Isn't it annoying how we settle for okay, instead of great? When we tell ourselves we're okay guess what, we are just okay, but when we tell ourselves, we're feeling great, guess what, we feel great!'

I gave him a friendly pat on his shoulder and turned to the rest of the group.

'Shall we begin?'

Everyone settled down in Ade and Lian's living room, they had arranged it well to accommodate us all. They had put a chair in front of the TV for me to address everyone.

'I would like to start by saying 'Thank you to Ade and Lian for hosting this evening in their lovely home. Secondly, 'Thanks to you all for sticking with the Ten Steps so far. I know Step One and Two take some getting used to, but when you sort them out, it's like a fog has cleared and the future looks brighter. That brings us to Step Three; our future.

Step Three is to determine what your goals in life are, who you would like to be, what you would like to achieve personally, financially, spiritually, health-wise, etc. In other words, looking to the future, what would you like your life to be like, now that you have left your past behind and have a little understanding about what your life is all about, and its purpose.'

Matt interrupted, *'I have to say, I am really having a problem with letting go of the past, forgiving and coming to terms with my past, my divorce, being made bankrupt… I know we talked about it before – but just look at me I'm a failure.'* Matt's head was down and his eyes were tearful. Ade put his arm around Matt.

Ade spoke softly to Matt. *'You can't keep on doing this to yourself. You're beginning to sound like a broken record. Stop beating yourself up mentally, that's exactly what we all do isn't it? Some people just do it to a greater degree. Have you heard the expression that your past does not equal your future?'*

I spoke up.

'Ade, that is so true. Matt, let's just look at some facts. Firstly, by which definition are you a failure? Failure is the greatest learning tool we have if we learn to use it. You see if we keep re-running in our minds our negative experiences we unconsciously hypnotise ourselves with those circumstances. You have to reprogram your mind, but you can't do that until you start looking forward and not backwards. Society teaches us to look backwards in a lot of cases and don't get me wrong, **it is important to reflect on the past, just don't live in the past.** Your mind is like a computer, if you put rubbish in, you get rubbish out. Who's in control of you? You or your past? Great question, isn't it? In fact, I'll ask it again, Who's in control of you? You or your past?

'All Step One is doing is getting you to see yourself from a different point of view. No amount of worrying, blaming or negative thinking is going to change where you're at today. You don't have to like the past, it's happened, accept it and get over it. We've witnessed a tsunami in the Philippines and Indonesia, a hurricane in New Orleans, earthquakes in Japan and Pakistan, and so many disasters and tragedies around the world. Every year there are disasters and tragedies but because they might be where you live you are not as affected till we all experienced Covid, the whole world into a lockdown you never could have imagined that… Just watch the BBC, CNN, Aljazeera any world news. Unfortunately, it takes a disaster or tragedy in the world for us as a people of the world to pull together with compassion. That's a real tragedy and yet those who have survived are trying to rebuild their lives. That's what I call a problem. Think about how many people die in the world every day from starvation and children dying from malnutrition – yet we complain about our lives.

'Did you know that 22,000 people die every day in Africa, that's 22,000 human lives! How many do you think die globally? In the Western world, we are spoiled, we take too much for granted, we see what we don't have, not what we have.

'Imagine if you had to walk five miles every day to get water just to drink… Would you swap their problems for yours? It would be interesting to see how quickly YOUR problems disappear. Stop feeling sorry for yourself. We need to get back to living in a world of gratitude.

'You are now at the beginning of a new chapter in your life. Matt, you have spent weeks and months going over and over what has happened to you, you are just in the habit of thinking that way. That's why you have to go over the exercises again and again until you have found your new positive beliefs, the new you! Just look at it this way, you are thirty-three years old; you have just had the worst two years of your life. Can you answer this Matt, two years from thirty-three years equals thirty-one good years? Are you going to write the next fifty-plus years of your life off because you have had a bad two years? Are you? I mean if you stop and think about it, it sounds stupid, doesn't it? If you lost in one of your pool tournaments, would you stop playing pool or get over it and work towards the next game?'

Matt looked at me in a thoughtful way. I could see that he was taking in everything that I was saying to him. He took a sip of tea from his mug, and set it down onto the table. He gave a little shrug of his shoulders and spoke

'You're right, Michael. I would get over it.'

'That's the spirit. Now, are you going to get over it or are you going to let your past beat you? The decision is yours! I can't help you, **the Ten Steps can't help you if you are going to live in the past, so Matt do you want to continue or call it quits?...'**

There was a pause for a moment. The room fell silent. Everyone held their breath waiting for Matt's reply.

'I'm going to try,' he said.

'No! trying is not good enough, there is no commitment in trying, trying is like saying I'm going to fail in advance. You are either going to do it or not. Only you can make that decision. Not once have I said that this was going to be easy. It will only work for you if you really want to change and move on. We will all support you, but you have to make that decision for yourself.'

I spoke to the rest of the group and said, 'Let's go out of the room and give Matt a few minutes to think it out. You have to decide if you are going to get over your past, **no matter what it takes** or whether you are going to carry on the way you are for the rest of your life, the decision is yours. The worst thing we can do, that most people do is listen and allow you to wallow in self-pity.

'Matt, I'm not trying to be hard on you but show you what you are doing to yourself, don't get me wrong we are all at some point guilty of holding on to the past. Give us a shout when you have decided.'

We all got up and went into the kitchen. Lian made us a fresh cup of tea then said *'You know, trying to sort out someone else's life, makes you look at your own. I don't know about you, but Ade and I need to make the decision to be totally committed to our new futures. It's easy saying it but taking action and actually doing it is something else.'*

Brianna spoke and said to me, *'Michael, don't you think you were too hard on Matt?'*

'Well, I'd rather be hard now and see him turn his life around, than watch him waste it wouldn't you?'

That statement made everyone think and re-evaluate their own commitments.

About ten minutes had passed when Matt knocked on the door. *'First, can I thank you for being patient with me. I've decided I'm committed to getting over my past and start working on the new me, but I will need your help and support.'*

Everyone reassured him. This incident seemed to have brought everyone closer together.

'Matt, we are here to help you go forward and not backwards. Okay, Step Three; are we ready?'

'Yes,' everyone replied in unison.

'The third step is about setting goals and clearly deciding who you would like to be. What do you want out of your life, family, career, spiritual and personal goals? What would you like to do or have? In other words, if you could describe your perfect world – What would it be?

By the way, there is no such thing as a perfect world; we can only strive for it. Don't forget your goals must be in harmony with what you want your life to represent and your purpose in life.

'Imagine you could have anything, what would you dare to wish for, to achieve, what one major goal would you want...?'

'Wow Michael, what a question,' said Matt.

'Picture yourself on one side of a riverbank; firstly, you have to decide you want to cross this river, because the other side is freedom, peace, happiness. Then all we have to do is to find a way to get across. If it were life or death, you would find a way across, wouldn't you?'

'Yes,' everyone said.

'So the new you, your goals, aspirations have got to be worth going after or you will never cross the river. Would you? If you are not prepared to make sacrifices for your goals they are just wishes. We're not just going to set the goal, but also do some exercises to qualify and identify your key goals. Learn to identify one major goal because that will take care of some of the smaller goals.

'Step Three is about setting clear goals and deciding what you want from your life. Isn't it amazing how we will plan a birthday or dinner party in detail, Christmas, a holiday but we never put the same effort into planning our lives for the next one, five or even ten years?'

Matt said *'Yes,* birthdays and parties are easy and simple to organise and execute. Our lives are more complicated...'

'Life is not complicated; it's just that we don't have simple plans to work to. That's what the Ten Steps are about. We are all born to win; born success-ful. Yet we are told not to dream big dreams. There is nothing wrong with thinking big, dreaming big if you are prepared to commit and pay the price for your goals. We are ridiculed more than encouraged. We are told what we can't do, rather than what we can do.

'The choices society gives us are to go to university, get a degree in something, serve an apprenticeship, marry someone rich, rob a bank, win the lottery. Probably 50% or more of people who go to school leave with an inferiority complex, lacking self-belief. Do you remember seeing your careers advisor? Basically, if you hadn't got the grades, you were written off. How can we let someone who has not been successful in business etc., tell a sixteen-year-old in their prime that they won't be good for anything? I'm not saying everyone is going to be successful but you don't take someone in their prime and shoot them down, do you. Now I am not criticising the education system, I'm just giving you another viewpoint. They try their best and we know how hard it must be for the teachers to stay focused when the kids are not interested, but what do we do? Do we give up or find another way?'

'Find another way, I suppose,' said Matt.

'Woah,' Ade said, *'I didn't realise you were this passionate Michael.'*

'Well, I am. I believe we are all individual and special. We all have a lot to offer and life is about realising our true potential. We live today, in the most abundant times, with limitless opportunities. There are so many examples of people from all walks of life, achieving and doing something with their lives, some have followed the orthodox route and some have been unconventional. Anything is possible if we only believe. Do you know it's easier to believe in someone else than it is to believe in yourself?

'There was a time in your life when you knew what you wanted in life, but that voice in your head said. "Don't be stupid, it's only you, you're not special."'

Lian replied. *'I hear that voice all the time talking to me saying that I can't do, could do that etc.'*

'We all hear that voice, that's why instead of listening to that negative internal voice, we need to confront it with the Ten Steps.'

'Talking of which, can we do the exercises now?' Ade interrupted

'Yes, Step Three… let me just get my notes. **Step Three is about making a**

list of all your goals and aspirations in life. It's important you know what you want out of your life and you'll never know until you put some thought into it.

Here's a quick story for you. There were three men in prison who had been wrongly imprisoned. They had been in prison for ten years and had a goal of escaping. One day the time came, they escaped and ended up lost in the jungle that surrounded the prison. They were free at last but now had to contend with the jungle. It was tougher than prison, at least in prison you were given three meals a day, a bed to sleep in. Now they were free and had to deal with insects, mosquitos, rain, poor shelter and no food. Three months passed by and it seemed that they had swapped one prison for another. One evening while they were exploring their surroundings, they found an old pot with an inscription on it. They couldn't read it; so they rubbed it clean to get a better look not being able to read the inscription, they opened the pot and out came a genie. The genie was so happy, 'I've been trapped for 200 years.' He said to the three men. 'You can all have one wish each, anything you want.

The first man said, "All I have thought about for the last ten years is I miss my family, my wife and children. I just want to be with them." The genie snapped his fingers and the first man disappeared back to his family. The second man said, "I want to be in the south of France, fast cars, plenty of money and a great life." The genie snapped his fingers and he went straight to France.

'The third guy went quiet. "I don't know what I want, I haven't really thought about it. I have just enjoyed the company of my two friends. I know what I want; I want to be with my two friends again.' The genie snapped his fingers and his two friends appeared instantly back in the jungle with him…'

Everyone laughed, *'It's not funny,'* said Brianna

'Well there is a good moral to this story,' I said. 'We need to know what we want from our lives or when the opportunity arises, we will miss it.'

Matt said, *'I liked the part when they escaped from the prison to the jungle, it reminded me of my situation. I feel like a prisoner of my circumstances and*

I've swapped one prison for another. That's what happens, you think you have escaped only to find out later that you are back in the same place.'

Everyone was amazed at Matt's explanation.

'You are right.' I said. 'You see they had a plan to escape, but didn't have a clear goal or what they were escaping to or what they were going to do once they were out of prison. What were they escaping to, a different type of prison. That's just like the saying, jumping out of the frying pan into the fire – that's what the third step is all about, establishing your goals and desires in life, so you have a clear direction at all times and you don't drift like a boat at sea with no rudder.'

Matt chipped in; *'I suppose you can say living life today is like living in a prison. You just have to choose which sort of prison you want to live in, one of pain and unhappiness or one of pleasure and satisfaction.'*

'That's another way of looking at it,' Ade said.

'Right, let's begin the exercises. But before we start let me explain what needs to be done. Step Three is to determine what your real goals in life are and these can be broken down into four main categories. The first is personal and family goals, these are what you want for yourself personally like a new car etc. and family goals may include for example; sending your children to private school, a new house etc. These are the goals that make you work. The next is business and career goals, you need this because you have to work and pay the bills to live and succeed, plus you also want to grow and be fulfilled. The third is self-improvement goals, these are the goals that will improve you and help make you a better you. Who we are has got us to where we are today, and who we become tomorrow will be down to improving on the person we are today.

**YOU TODAY + SELF IMPROVEMENT
(NEW SKILLS, HABITS & THINKING)**

=

**IMPROVED YOU OF TOMORROW (SUCCESSFUL, BECOMING
THE BEST YOU, YOU CAN BE & MORE FULFILLED)**

And lastly, spiritual and holistic goals…your beliefs, your purpose. This is how it works; your career goals and business goals are what you want, for you and your family and personal goals are why you are doing it, your spiritual and holistic goals are your purpose, your self-improvement goals are who you need to become to achieve it. It is important that all your goals are in harmony with your purpose in life.

'When you make your list, make sure that you put down everything. Imagine that genie asking you for your top 100 wishes. What would they be? Write them down, even if it sounds silly, we will sort them out later. Are you ready, you have just fifteen minutes. This is just to get you started, you will need more time at home.

I got up from my seat in front of the TV and asked Ade if I could go and pop the kettle on to make everyone a drink. He was engrossed in writing his list, but looked up, smiled, and gave me a thumbs-up.

Do exercise 7 at the end of the chapter

'Your 15 minutes are up.' I said as I walked back into the living room.

'Really? Gosh, that went fast,' said Ade.

'Your tea and coffee are ready. You know, I couldn't help but think how different we all are. Everyone had a different combination of tea, milk, sugar, sweeteners etc.'

'We are all individuals,' Matt said, jokingly.

We all laughed.

'I haven't finished,' said Brianna and Lian.

'That's ok, ladies. The last fifteen minutes was just to get you started. It's going to take time. You need to find time and make time. Once you have your goals, I will show you how to prioritise them.

'Have you heard the saying, that life is a journey and not a destination? Have you also heard that life is not a dress rehearsal? This is it, so it's important we do our best to enjoy the journey as much as possible. That's why we must go over and over the Ten Steps and act on them.

'You see by using the goals that you set, you begin to control your journey in life, instead of someone else controlling your life. You can be the driver in your car or the passenger. As the driver, you have total control over your destinations. As a passenger, you go where the driver goes and if the driver is not in harmony with where you want to go, they take you where they want to go.

'Your goals are the steering wheel guiding you safely to your destination. Imagine driving with no steering wheel, what would happen?'

'You would crash,' said Matt.

'Guess what happens when we don't have goals?'

'We crash,' said Ade.

'That's right.' I said.

Goals help us control the directions we are moving in. Goals help us to activate our success mechanism.

Lian replied, *'I know what you are saying but it's not easy, is it?'*

'Life isn't easy is it, whoever said it was? Life is a continuous series of challenges and how we respond to them determines the life we have. Our goals help us to stay in control. I believe one of the greatest feelings you have as a person, is when you feel in total control of your life, isn't it? **Your degree of happiness and fulfilment is directly related to the amount of control you have in your life.**

'A good example is when you play a sport or game and you are winning, you are in control, and you feel really good. Well, that's how you will feel when you start chasing and achieving your goals. As you start achieving you need to replace them with new goals. The world is yours if you can see it that way. **There is a quote that I like by the author H. M. Tomlinson — 'If we can change our thoughts, we can change the world.'**

Right, the next step is to go over every goal you have written and put a date by it as when you would like it to be achieved. A goal without a date is a wish. The date gives us focus and urgency and propels you towards the goal.

So go back to your exercise and add the dates, again don't think too hard at this stage as you will have to review them again. I will give you five minutes...'

Go to exercise 7 and add dates to goals to be achieved by (exercise 7e)

I sat down with the rest of the group and I used the five minutes to review my goals too...

'Is everyone finished?'

'Sort of...' they mumbled.

'It's not easy putting a date next to your goal is it?' said Ade.

'It's not, but a date is better than no date. Now it's important that the date to achieve this is reasonable and attainable. It's just like saying; I'm going from £20,000 a year to £100,000 a year in twelve months, that's pushing it.

'Your goals must be believable and achievable otherwise you won't work towards them. They should have at least a 50/50 chance of you achieving them.

'So the next step *(exercise 7f)* is to review your goals again and again and ask yourself, do they have a 50/50 chance? Put a Y for Yes and an N for No by the side of the goal.

'Go over each goal and question, do you really desire this goal, is it important to you? Are you prepared to make sacrifices for this goal? How would you benefit from it? Are you prepared to come out of your comfort zone for this goal?

'You will only work towards a goal that has a meaning to you, that you desire. The rest are all wishes

'The ones that you truly desire please put a 'D' by them and then rewrite your new master goal list with the ones you desire (Exercise 8)

'The next step…

Brianna exclaimed, *'Stop! Wait a minute Michael, you're going too fast'*

'I'm sorry guys, I'm excited for us all and maybe got a little carried away. I think that's a good note to finish on and don't forget to rewrite your goals.'

As we all stood up to leave, everyone thanked Ade and Lian for their hospitality. Brianna said that we should meet at her place the following evening at the same time.

'One last word for the evening – make sure that you spend time on your goals. We will be moving onto Step Four tomorrow…'

'What's Step Four about?' Ade asked.

'You'll find out tomorrow. Let's take it one step at a time.'

CHAPTER FIVE

Steps Four and Five
Step Four: Establish the help and support you need to achieve your goals
Step Five: Believe in yourself and your goals

It was Friday and another week had been and gone. I had found it hard to concentrate on work this week. This had been a life-changing experience for me. We have life-changing days, life-changing weeks, life-changing months and the biggest of all, life-changing years. However, I am a little scared about the future and where it's going to take me. Talking about the future, Isabella was coming home tomorrow; getting Isabella to understand and be supportive of how I was making changes to my life – no to OUR lives, was going to be my biggest challenge since undertaking the Ten Steps. I was going to find out if she was to be by my side, or if she wanted to go her own way. We had talked on the phone and I told her a little about the steps, but she didn't seem to be at all understanding of what I was saying to her.

I looked up from my desk and saw Brianna standing there. I was so wrapped up in my thoughts that I hadn't even noticed her.

'Hi Brianna, I said. Sorry, have you been there long?'

'Well, as a matter of fact, yes, I've been standing here trying to get your attention for a minute or so… you just seemed to be on another planet,' she said jokingly.

'I'm sorry Brianna, I was just thinking.'

'I know what you mean; I sometimes find myself doing the same thing too…'

'Are you ok?' I asked as Brianna looked a little concerned about something.

'Well, I'm a bit nervous about Matt coming around to my house this evening. I know it sounds silly, but I don't really know him…'

'I'm sure it will be ok, Brianna. But if you're really not happy – then we will have to make alternative arrangements. I don't want you to feel under any pressure.'

Brianna bit her lip and thought for a moment. *'I suppose I'm overreacting,'* she said. *'Just ignore me; we'll carry on as planned.'*

'Are you sure?'

'Yes I am, I'll see you at seven o'clock.'

Five o'clock came, and we all went home. Whilst I completed a few more bits of housework, I couldn't stop thinking about how I was going to approach the subject of the ten steps with Isabella, and how we could have a constructive discussion when she came back.

I was the first to arrive at Brianna's flat and made sure that she was okay.

'You're early!' Brianna said

'Yes, I am. I just wanted to make sure that you feel alright.'

'Yes, I am. In fact, I'm looking forward to tonight'

'You've really got your home looking nice,' I said. There were lavender scented candles lit around the living room and a plate with some cheese and crackers, 'This is really lovely, Brianna.'

'Thanks. Would you like a glass of wine?'

'Yes please, I'd love a glass of red if you have any?'

As Brianna was pouring the wine, the doorbell went.

Brianna looked up and asked me if I would mind answering it.

I opened the door and let Ade and Lian in. As I helped them off with their coats, Brianna shouted through from the front room asking if they would like a glass of wine too. They both replied *'White please'* as we walked into the room where Brianna was.

We all sat down with our drinks and a plate each with a few crackers and cheese on them.

As we sat chatting I noticed that it was ten past seven.

'I wonder where Matt has got to?'

Just then there was a knock at the door. It was Matt. *'Sorry I'm late – I got a bit lost.'*

'No worries,' said Brianna. She handed Matt a glass of wine and some nibbles, and he joined the rest of us.

'You have a lovely place, Brianna,' said Matt admiringly.

Brianna smiled and thanked him for the compliment.

'Are we ready to get started?'

'Yes,' replied everyone.

'First of all, let me ask everyone, have you followed the first three steps?'

Ade was the first to speak; *'I feel like I have been in a time warp. I know now what I want in life, what my life is all about. I have just got to go out and get it. I just think that it is sad that we are groomed from birth for two things. One is to get a job so you can live within a structure and the other is to get married or settle down with someone. I now realise **there is a third dimension which is to try and find your purpose in life and go for it**. We are born to win, whatever the circumstances. All we have to do is decide what we want to win at and we* *can spend the rest of our lives winning, Just by setting our goals, evolving and not living within the confines of society's beliefs.'*

'Some things just can't be sorted out overnight,' I said, that's why the Ten Steps are a process that needs to be repeated for the rest of our lives, because you are changing every day and your perspective in life changes too. You will see things differently in time. What you need to do is go over your notes again, but stop fighting the information, digest it and let your brain come to its own conclusion. It is important that you come to terms with your own beliefs because they control your future. Anyway, let me move on.'

Step Four is about us establishing the people's help, support, motivation, discipline, organisations, books, YouTube channels, podcasts etc – anything that will help make your plans and goals work.

'For example, let me take my goal of earning £75,000 per year. Whatever I am going to do is going to require commitment and time, so I need to get the support of Isabella. One of the greatest pressures you can have is not to have your partner support you in your goal. It makes it twice as hard. I'm going to need to read books to know what direction I want to go in. I need to find someone already more successful than me; earning the salary that I want and using them as my role model or mentor. I need to build a reference group of successful people who will point me in the right direction. Listen to some motivational and educational materials, Podcasts there is a wide variety of information out there. It's a great opportunity to get a one to one, by listening to successful business people, how they work, and learning from them, how they achieved their success, not to mention their secret to success. What you get is years of hard work, experience and wisdom distilled down into either a set of videos, audio tracks or podcasts. It's like going through a short education course in success.

'We are back again to the point; you only get out what you put in. You see there are two things in life; **knowing what to do** and **doing what you know**. Without the support group of people, books and any educational material it becomes difficult to sustain focus and commitment.

'A great place to start is YouTube or go to some seminars, and speak to an entrepreneur. Most entrepreneurs and top managers love telling their stories of success and giving advice, especially as you remind them of what they were like starting out.'

'*Where do I begin?*' said Matt.

'It doesn't matter, so long as you begin right now. Think of tidying a room, it doesn't matter where you start so long as you start. The more information you get, the more intelligent your decisions will become. Only you can find out what's right for you. Remember we are all born successful, it's just between birth and twenty we start to doubt ourselves. It's all in the mind.

'Matt, look at your goals, pick one career goal, one personal goal, one family goal and go and do your research. Once you have done your research add any extra requirements to your plan of action.

'Do you all understand Step Four?' There was a pause,

'*Well, yes I think.*' Ade said. '*Let me get this right. Let's take my goal of a new house. I know what house I want and where I want it. What I need to establish is, who are the people, knowledge, help etc., I need to buy the house. Is that right Michael?*'

'Yes, it is.'

'*So let me see, I'll need to find out more about the different types of mortgages, what income I'll need to get the mortgage. I'll need the help of my employer or new employer. We need to work out the deposit required; we need help to fix our house up so as to get the maximum back.*'

'That's right, you're getting the idea. Now, go and see a financial advisor or a building society/bank and ask them what you will need. Get two or three opinions. Once you know the people, groups, institutions etc. that can help you, it will speed the process up. Step Four is a simple and straightforward step. So let's just quickly recap on what we have learned so far.'

Step One was about accepting where you are at today, and who you are today, don't look to the past, don't blame anyone. This is you, today, and **today is your new beginning**.

Step Two is establishing your own opinions on what life is all about i.e. your purpose in life and how that affects your life and what you want to do with it and your spiritual beliefs.

Step Three is getting your dream list together. What are your goals? What would you like to do with your life? And then qualifying them to make sure you desire them and thus, are really important to you. In other words, turning your dreams into reality.

Step Four is establishing the help and support you will need to achieve your goals. This is like a business plan we're putting together. The only difference is that it's a business plan for our lives.

'*I never thought of it that way,*' said Ade

'Have you all done your exercises so far?'

'*Yes we have,*' replied Lian, Ade and Matt.

Brianna let out a long sigh and said, '*I have just been so tired, I am behind on a couple of the exercises.*'

'Well don't beat yourself up, but do make the time as soon as possible to do your exercises. **Stay with the program**. This is serious business; it's planning your new life.

'*I know,*' said Brianna, '*... You don't have to preach to the converted.*'

'The next six steps won't be as demanding; in fact, I am going to quickly cover Step Five now, while we have time on our sides. Is that okay with everyone?' They all agreed.

'Now before we go into Step Five, let's just do Step Four and the corresponding exercise quickly. Can you take your goals and make a list of all the people, organisations, books, audio materials etc. that will help you to achieve your goals. You have fifteen minutes. If it's okay Brianna, I'll make everyone a cup of tea.' I made everyone a quick drink while they finished off Step Four.

Go to exercises for steps four and five

'Okay, are you all finished?'

'You have to be joking?' said Lian. *'This needs thinking out a lot more'*

'I know what you mean,' said Brianna and Matt.

'I will give you another five minutes otherwise you will have finish it tomorrow.'

Five minutes went by. 'Right! Let's do Step Five'

We have already talked about our beliefs, but the reason we are specifically covering this at this stage is – if your beliefs are against your goals, then you will fail to achieve your goals. If you don't believe in yourself, you desire better, you have to get it.'

'Step Five is about belief. It's about belief in yourself, your life, your goals and your future. I'd like to start this session with a question. Why shouldn't you be successful? Why shouldn't you have a good life, nice home, car etc.? Why shouldn't you be happy? Why shouldn't you have a high opinion of yourself? That is so long as you are not arrogant about it. Why should you accept your struggles in life? Why?…'

'Your beliefs in life are like a pair of glasses you see the world through. If you have limiting, negative beliefs, then your life is limited and negative, if you have positive beliefs then your life is happier, more positive and more optimistic.'

'Do you remember the story of the man who lost his job, and his wife pretended she had won money on the lottery? Well, let's think about this, although the story was false, he believed it to be true and acted accordingly.

You see your beliefs control your attitude, your attitude controls your actions and your actions are a reflection of whether you are fulfilled and happy. One of our main challenges in life is we have true and false beliefs that control our self-concepts about ourselves. Which in turn controls our lives. A lot of these beliefs we never questioned as to why we believe in them, where do they come from? That's part of what we are doing with the Ten Steps. Let me give you an example. Some people today have a belief system that the world we live in today is terrible, ruthless, not like the good old days. Well if your beliefs have it that the good old days were the good times, and today is the bad times, then all you will do is highlight all the negatives there are in the world today and you end up living a life of pessimism. If those are the kind of thoughts that you subscribe to, then your beliefs would be that happiness is in the past and sadness is in the present and the future.

'You only need to get a history book and see that the world has always been a troubled place to live in, that's why we need guidance. Every decade has had its good points and bad points. You just have to watch a few of the old movies like *Spartacus, Gladiator, A Bridge Too Far, Saving Private Ryan* etc., the list goes on.

'Those are some great classic films,' Matt said.

'Yes they are and we can learn a lot from them, but would you have liked to live in those times?

'We are now living in the best times ever, and everyone has an opportunity, especially in the Western world.

'Now, before we go any further, I'd just like to point out that I'm not knocking the good old days. The good old days were very good for some and I bet some people had some fantastic times. We just need to move on and become current, move into the 21st century. **The world is evolving, are you evolving with it?**

'I am not saying that the world we live in today is perfect either. What I am saying is that we look at the positives in the world today and continue to strive to make it a better place. As Michael Jackson sang in his song 'Man in the Mirror', *I'm starting with the man in the mirror, I'm asking him to change his ways... If you want to make the world a better place – take a look at yourself, and then make a change.'* There are so many songs you can draw strength from, another one I like is 'The Greatest Love of All' by George Benson; the list is endless.

'Your belief system can keep you alive or kill you. How many stories have you heard now of people who have been diagnosed with cancer, given six weeks to live and have lived for another three, four, five-plus years? Some have even cured themselves. For example, the lady called Ruth Heidrich literally took her life into her own hands and proactively cured herself of her diagnosis of breast, bone and lung cancer after refusing chemotherapy and radiation. The doctors don't understand what happened, all they know is that cancer has gone. I will go as far as to say that **the quality of your life is down to your beliefs. Positive beliefs; you are a happy person and negative beliefs; you are an unhappy person. You either have reasons to be successful or excuses to fail. Your happiness is controlled by your beliefs.**

'You are the only one out of a million sperm cells that made it. You are special. You have a unique DNA, you are **'born to win'** but to realise it you must **believe.**

'Do you remember the film *Apollo 13*?'

'Yes,' they said.

'Well do you remember the scene when they discover a problem with the air filtration system not removing the carbon dioxide? So the astronauts were going to die in space because there would not be enough oxygen left to keep them alive on the return journey back down to earth. Do you remember that crucial point?'

'Yes we do.'

'The staff at NASA were giving up on the mission when the director of operations, Gene Kranz, slammed his fist on the desk and told everyone **"Failure is not an option**. I have never lost an American in space and I'm sure not going to lose one now, so get back to work and find a solution."

'Think of all the scientists, technicians and highly trained people at NASA that were about to give up when one man, the director of operations, who believed there was a way decided that **failure was simply not an option**. The power of belief is amazing, isn't it?'

'Yes it is,' the group replied.

'We have all had experiences when you think about it where our beliefs have carried us. Stop and think about that for a moment...'

'When you embark on this new journey to your new life, you have to have the belief that "Failure is not an option", do we all agree to this?'

I looked at the faces in front of me and they were all nodding in agreement.

'Yes,' they all said together.

'If you surround yourself with positive people, you'll become positive. If you associate with winners, you too will become a winner. But only if you believe that you are a winner. You are born to win. **Are you sick and tired of being sick and tired?** You are going to do something with your life now, do you believe in yourself, you have a legacy to offer the world and before your time on earth is over, you will stand proud and say **'This I have done, This I have done' Stand tall, believe in yourself and then put on your overalls and go to work. When your beliefs are strong enough, your beliefs become your faith!'**

Life is 10% what happens and 90% how you respond to it and how you respond depends on your belief system at the time. Let me give you an example, I applied for a promotion and I didn't get it. Deep inside I don't think I was good enough for the job anyway. So when I didn't get it, I wasn't surprised. Has that happened to any of you?'

'That's happened several times to me,' said Ade.

Matt chimed in. 'Me too.'

'One of the biggest limiting beliefs as a person is "We are not good enough" so when anything negative happens, our core response is that we are not good enough. So we're not surprised.

'Where do our beliefs come from? They come from our self-concepts about ourselves and our self-concepts come from our true or false experiences in life and our experiences in life starting from our childhood. From when we were babies, how we were brought up, the environment we lived in, how we were treated by our parents, family, teachers, friends etc.' How we were loved…

'So it's all my mum and dad's fault?' said Matt.

'Stop right there. This is not guilt or a blame trip. You will never free yourself and go forward if you start to apportion blame or use guilt. It's not your parents' fault and it's not society. **What's happened has happened. Learn from it and move on. Use your past to understand why you are the person you are today and use today to shape the person you want to be tomorrow.**

'If you want to blame your parents then you need to blame your grandparents and their parents and so on and so on. Eventually, you will be left with two choices; one, I can't change because that's my heritage and two, now I know what caused the problem, I can change. Don't assassinate your childhood and negative experiences you had because some of those experiences have shaped you and they are what has made you who you are today. Remember what we said, **Life is about evolving through our experiences and using our experiences to shape us in the path of our beliefs and goals.'**

'I don't want to get too deep, but we need to understand that we all have got a few limiting beliefs we need to work on. The biggest cure for your limiting beliefs is to love yourself and approve of yourself. To forgive yourself and everyone from your past. I know it sounds silly and simple but that's what you have to do. That's why Step One is so important, accept who you are and where you are today as a beginning.

'I'm not asking you to be vain about yourself; I'm asking you to like YOU, to love YOU, to approve of YOU. Approving of yourself is so important. If there's anything in the past you don't like about yourself, forgive yourself, let go and seek the new you. Do you know what's sad? We as a human race spend most of our time developing a new model car, computer, stereo, new décor in our house, the latest phone etc., all aimed at how we look on the outside, but little time is spent on our mindset, our beliefs and how we feel on the inside. That's the real change. We have no time for developing the new you. All change begins from within.'

'Imagine that every year as a human being on your birthday, you had to display before your friends and family the new you, your new values and beliefs, new goals etc. Just like a yearly fashion or motor show. **Imagine what your aspirations would be, if you had twelve months to prepare and show the world, this is the new me. Spiritually, mentally, physically, career, hobbies, relationships** etc. Imagine? Well, we don't have to imagine anymore because we've got the power, we are all born successful, we just need motivation and guidance – and that's what the Ten Steps are all about.'

'You know what,' said Brianna. *'That is such a great idea. It allows you to get rid of parts about you, habits etc. that you don't like and explore and develop the new you. Imagine if we did that, you would actually evolve into a better you.'*

'Now I like that,' said Ade

'You have a story to tell and this story isn't finished until your heart packs up, so tell your story. Believe in yourself, you are **born to win**.

'Now I want you to repeat after me, **'I am born to win,'**

'I am born to win,' they murmured.

Louder: 'I am born to win'

'I AM BORN TO WIN!' they all said in unison, with big smiles on their faces.

'This is exciting and motivating… and probably a good time to start to wrap up the evening. Right before we finish there is an exercise to do first, what do you think Step Five is about?'

Matt said; *'Step Five to me, is about believing that I am born to win and to not let my negative limiting beliefs get the better of me.'*

'I couldn't have said that better myself Matt,' said Ade

'Right, let's all repeat that to ourselves: "Step Five is about believing that I am born to win and to not let my negative limiting beliefs get the better of me."

'We need beliefs that will empower us, make us stronger and more confident. It's important that whenever you look in the mirror, the person you see in the reflection is someone you like and respect. Think of what you have been through in your life so far. That's an achievement. Remember, use where you are today as your new beginning. Make a positive list of yourself, pick your top ten and read them every day.

'The easiest way to start changing any limiting belief is to take them one by one, write it down, and rewrite it in a positive way. Let me give you an example. Let me see, here's a simple one… I'm hopeless at cooking. Well, how many times do you think I have said that to myself? Thousands of times and every time I repeat to myself, I am reaffirming my negative beliefs. That is, I am not good at cooking. How can you become good at something that you keep telling yourself that you are not good at? It's impossible isn't it?'

'I see what you mean,' said Ade.

'Your subconscious mind, which carries out all the orders from your conscious mind, cannot differentiate which is positive or negative, good or bad, it just acts on the instructions it is given. So when I try to cook, there's that little voice in my head going, you know you are no good at this so why bother. It's going to taste awful and so on and so on, so you make some mistakes and even when I cook a good meal and people compliment me on my cooking, I usually reply with the remark, thank you, but it really isn't that good, I got lucky etc. So you can see how difficult it will be for me to be a good cook when I keep telling myself over and over that I'm not a good cook.'

'To change is simple, but not easy as you are now having to break some bad habits. To accomplish the change requires hard work and discipline. To change I'm not good at cooking is simple. I need to tell myself, many times over, that I am a good cook, in fact, I am a great cook. Now I've got to start believing that I am a great cook. Then I need to get some help and advice on cooking and then I need to practise. All I have to do is find one or two dishes to get good at and then add another one or two until before I know it, I could have ten or twenty special dishes. At this point, being a good cook will simply be part of the new me.'

'Does that mean that you are going to cook for us one of these days?' said Matt, turning to the rest of the group and winking.

'No, I'm not you cheeky man. I was just giving you an example.' I shook my head and laughed.

'You know Michael, I've enjoyed tonight but it doesn't half feel like I am back at school, with all these exercises we have to do. Don't get me wrong, I'm not com-plaining, I'm just making an observation,' said Matt.

'You're right; **we're back in the real school of life' the school of your life, your future, your happiness, your success in whatever you choose. The question is, are you worth it? Only you can answer that question.**

'When you get home what you need to do is go back to our first exercise and review your positive beliefs, negative/limiting beliefs and see if any have changed and redo the exercise. Then finishing by reaffirming your positive beliefs in a positive present tense range of sentences e.g. I am a great cook.'

Everyone stood up and was ready to leave

'Don't forget to do your exercises and keep recapping on what we have done. The more times you recap, the more it becomes part of you, the new you. One important exercise, I want you to do is to start looking in the mirror, look straight in the eyes, pause for a second to admire yourself and say *"I am born to win, I am a good person, every experience I encounter is a success I believe in myself. I approve of myself."* Make your own positive affirmations up and at first, you will find this very awkward, but don't give up, it's the old you fighting the new you.

When you have negative thoughts, challenge them and where they have come from in the first place. Believe in yourself, you are special and remember that you are worth fighting for. Some of us have more belief in our football teams than we do in ourselves. **If you are going to hero-worship, start with yourself.** Appreciating yourself is not being big-headed, bragging is.'

We all thanked Brianna for her kind hospitality and just before we left, Matt reminded us of his address so that we could meet there for the next chapter.

We agreed to take the following evening off so that everyone could spend the time going over what we had already learned.

Ade and Lian approached me outside. Ade put his hand on my shoulder, looked me directly in the eye and said *'I have never seen you so inspired like that before, you had so much energy. Did you notice how quiet the group was when you were talking? You really believe in these Ten Steps don't you?'*

'Yes, I do. I feel like telling the world, but I'm afraid of being rejected, criticised and people questioning who I am. What qualification or experience have I got to proclaim these Ten Steps? That's why I understand that the Ten Steps are not for everyone, only for the people like us who are at a crossroads in our lives that want to change, that want to listen, learn and apply. I know Brianna, Matt and the both of you are keen, but I feel it is my duty to try and reach as many people as possible. Some of us need a helping hand or push to start our success journey. Can I do that, can we do that, I don't know? Time will tell.'

Lian in a soft voice said *'Michael don't doubt yourself, we believe in you, you can do it, I know you can, especially with the help of the Ten Steps.'* And on that note, we all went our separate ways.

When I got home, I was still energised by the meeting and the kind words that Ade and Lian had said. I decided to do my finishing touches towards the house. Isabella and the boys were due home tomorrow afternoon. I wanted to be ready; it was going to be a big day for me. I missed them all so much and I could only but hope that Isabella would embrace the Ten Steps, if she would, it could change our lives forever...

CHAPTER SIX

Isabella's return

It was Saturday. The crisp spring day dawned as light poured through my window, bringing with it new hopes and aspirations. Isabella, Emilio and Jason were coming home from their holiday with Isabella's parents. I continued to contemplate over the conversation I was going to have with Isabella tonight. We had spoken daily on the phone and I had briefly explained what had happened to me with the Ten Steps, but unfortunately, this soon escalated into an argument over the phone; *'It's a load of nothing. How are we going to pay the mortgage and bills…You're just not facing reality Michael,'* she said.

The problem now was that I was facing the reality with the Ten Steps and how I had changed over these last seven days. I now had a different view and focus on life. This was going to be tough as Isabella was as stubborn as I was and I knew if we could not see eye to eye, our marriage could potentially be over, and that was the very last thing I wanted. I understood that we couldn't go forward if we continued to look backwards. I had to sit down with Isabella and ask her to read the Ten Steps. The survival of our marriage would depend on this… I didn't want to lose Isabella. We needed to set some big goals together about our future – and it was OUR future. I just couldn't imagine what life would be like without Isabella. She was the love of my life.

Isabella had always rejected these so-called 'motivational tools'; in fact, she had become more pessimistic over the last couple of years. Was she ready to change? Was she at that crucial point in life for a change in direction? Well nobody said it was going to be easy. I love Isabella, it's just that we have allowed the pressures of life to get to us and we have focused on the negatives and not the positives.

I decided that I would put some love and effort into cooking her a romantic dinner, crack open a bottle of wine, and discuss the Ten Steps with her. I also had to broach the subject that I had had meetings at our home. Isabella wasn't happy about other people visiting the house without it being spotless.

This is going to have to be a good dinner. Our love was worth fighting for. I had to be strong for both of us.

I had some breakfast and did some work around the house as I wanted Isabella to see that our home looked clean and tidy so that she felt relaxed coming home.

It looked and smelled lovely. I took a vase out of the cupboard and arranged some daffodils and roses that I cut from the garden. I plumped up all of the cushions on the sofa and put some kindling into the log basket so that we could have a cosy fire this evening.

It was such a crisp and fresh day that I felt like going for a walk to get some country air. I decided to spend an hour or two in a lovely little place called Hartington which is in the Peak District. There was a sweet little cafe there that sold homemade scones and served them with their own clotted cream made and churned from the cows that they kept. Then I would make my way to the airport.

It was a beautiful spring day and the sun was casting its golden rays all around. The blossom on the trees looked delicious in shades of pinks and creams. Isabella and I had done this walk several times with Jason and Emilio, but I hadn't taken this route on my own. As I walked to the top of the hill, looking down on the valley below, I began to feel that natural high of mind, body and soul, all in harmony with nature. I stopped to take in the view of the cows grazing, lambs jumping and playing on the ground and felt peace and tranquillity across the gentle slopes. I couldn't help but think what a wonderful world we live in, Mother Nature at her best. It's amazing how the sun can change the view of how you see a place; the sun shines twenty-four hours a day and never goes out. It's just the clouds or should I say our negative thoughts that get in the way of seeing how wonderful life is. We need to keep up with the sun and rise above the clouds and negativity.

We can't change the weather, but we can change our thoughts. Every day is a beautiful day. **We need to develop our own sun – or should I say attitude – towards life.**

Your attitude is like the sun or the clouds. Some days it's sunny and sometimes it's cloudy.

Our goals and our purpose in life are just like the sun shining down, bringing a new meaning and vitality to how we see, how we act and how we behave. No goals: no sunshine… food for thought.

I love spring; everywhere seems to be bursting with energy. Spring had come early; March had been one of the mildest for thirty years and some daffodils had already started to appear and come out. I feel like a daffodil just getting ready to bloom. I was just beginning to come out.

I walked across the fields, back into the country lane, when I came to the bottom of the hill, which marked the halfway point for my walk. I was heading back, as it was a circular walk. Around the bend at the bottom of the hill, there was small woodland – carpeted with hundreds of snowdrops and a few of the daffodils and crocuses in bloom. It was like an artist's palette of nature. Whites, yellows, purples, oranges… What an incredible sight. I had been here many times; it was lovely to see the old farmhouse and outbuildings that had been made into cottages. I was in the valley now, which provided a new vista of rolling hills. This was definitely a beautiful day, one to remember. The Ten Steps had changed the way I looked at life.

As I carried on my thoughts drifted off again. **Life is like the four seasons; winter, spring, summer and autumn**, the only difference being that there are no time limits on how long you remain in any of these seasons in the game of life. What's exciting is that we have the power to change which season we are in, whenever you wish. 'What season am I in? I thought for a moment… well I definitely have been in the winter and looking back now, I kept myself there with my negative thoughts, but I am in spring now thanks to the Ten Steps.'

Winter is feeling sorry for yourself, being trapped in your negative thoughts, blaming others for your own problems. It's being stuck in a rut, no goals, no future, fed up with life, remaining introverted, being stressed, worrying, feeling angry, hateful, spiteful, depressed... the list goes on! What a horrible place to live in and I have been doing that for the last few years.

Spring is when you reinvent yourself, with new positive beliefs, goals, a game plan for your life, a strong belief in your future. It is where you plant the seeds for success. It's where you see your plans beginning to take shape. Spring is new energy just waiting to burst out.

Summer is where your plans blossom; it's where you start succeeding on your goals and plans. You begin to enjoy the rewards of your hard work. This is where you have fun and enjoy life. It's about good times and looking forward to every new day.

Autumn is where we begin to stop reinventing ourselves, we stop evolving and we become bored with ourselves and life. We stop doing the things we used to do; we are slower to respond to situations. We have no new goals and we allow ourselves to be distracted and influenced negatively. This is when we take our eye off the ball and begin to take things for granted with a lack of attention to detail.

The four seasons of life, I have lived in them all and now I know through the help of the Ten Steps, whenever I get into autumn, I can review my goals, reinvent myself and go back to spring or summer. I am in control now, I am in control, I am in control... What a wonderful feeling... In fact, if we stop and think about it, the four seasons concept applies to so many situations.

In fact, my relationship and marriage with Isabella are like the four seasons. We are definitely in winter now and the Ten Steps were hopefully going to get us back into spring. Spring is the season where romance begins. I remember when Isabella and I first met, the things we did, how happy we were...

The changes from spring to summer to autumn to winter are very subtle, that's why we don't see them coming. I definitely hate winter; all the nagging and the arguing. How could something that was so beautiful become so sour? I suppose this is what the Ten Steps are about; if we don't keep review-ing and resetting our goals together, we grow out of harmony with each other and our needs change. Seasons will change and before we know it we are back in winter. **We could say that in fact, the winter season is a wake-up call to the reality of life if you don't nurture it.**

We can apply the four seasons methods to anything. You can apply it to work. I'm in autumn now at work, I need to shape up fast and get back to spring.

As I was pondering on the seasons and how we can reflect upon them in everyday life, I realised that I had almost finished my walk. I began to think about my scones with jam and clotted cream when I came to the part of my journey where the underground spring waters from the hills came out to form a stream that fed into the River Dove. The water was flowing fast into the river and the river overflowed down the lane. Another thought… **Life is like a river; it has to flow**, it has to go some-where and when we stop the flow, the water becomes stagnant and hor-rible. This is what happens when we stop the flow of life. What's life all about? Life is about endlessly realising your true potential. I felt so alive right now at that moment. The fresh air, the beauty and wonder of nature and a new me gave me something to smile about. This was definitely an enlightening walk.

My thoughts quickly returned their focus towards Isabella. I was only a few hours from picking her up from the airport with the twins. How I've missed them all. I had definitely changed in the last seven days. A feeling of anxiety slowly washed over me… but what was I worried about? I desperately wanted to share how I felt with Isabella, but would she listen? Would she understand?

Lunch was great, the scones were delightful. They are freshly baked every day, with clotted cream… what a treat. I made my way to Manchester air-port. The flight was on time. Isabella looked sun-kissed and very beautiful. Her chestnut hair had been lightened in streaks by the sun and her green eyes shone. She looked happy and relaxed. Emilio and Jason were walking together and laughing. The boys saw me and they both raced over and into my open arms. I had missed them so much. Isabella was still pushing the trolley towards me, I looked at her and she smiled at me until her nose creased and her eyes crinkled. She looked as though she was very pleased to see me. I walked up to Isabella and gave her a big kiss and a hug. 'I've missed you all so much,' I uttered. I didn't realise it, I thought I had been so caught up with the events of the last seven days, I had forgotten how much Isabella, Emilio and Jason truly meant to me and how much I had missed them.

I collected the suitcases and bags and we went home. Isabella was surprised when we returned to the house. The lawns had been cut; the house was tidy and there was no washing or ironing to do. I had even prepared dinner for us all.

'*Are you ok Michael?*' she said.

'Yes, of course my love' I replied, 'I just wanted to make sure we had time tonight to go through what happened while you were away. A lot has happened.'

Isabella turned and gave 'that' look and said, '*A lot happened…well I can't wait to find out.*'

Isabella unpacked and got the boys bathed and ready for bed while I continued finishing the dinner.

I had made healthy pizzas from tortillas, with ham and pineapple toppings for the boys. These were their favourites. They ate them and went to watch a childrens' programme while Isabella sat and had a glass of red wine as I finished cooking dinner.

When dinner was almost ready Isabella took the boys up to bed. There was no resistance as they were tired from their long journey from Spain back to the UK.

Isabella and I sat down to eat; I had prepared salmon in a prawn sauce with a selection of vegetables and pineapple upside-down cake. All accompanied by a bottle of our favourite red wine.

The stage was set. I started by explaining the chain of events from the previous week. How I had come home from the airport feeling miserable and stressed, feeling sorry for myself.

'I heard this voice talking to me, I know this may sound crazy but that's the only way I can explain what happened that evening. I spent the whole night, writing out the Ten Steps and since then, I'm a changed man. What I mean is my outlook on life has changed. I feel more positive about who I am, about us and where we are going. I know why we have arguments. We've been caught up in the rat race, keeping up appearances, paying bills, surviving and not being able to look to the future. **We have become worriers; a new breed of people in the 21st century**. We worry about everything and in the end as a result; we focus on the negatives in our lives.'

Go to Chapter 6 exercises

'Life is about evolving and learning how to make the right choices to get you what you want. However, it's also about knowing what you want in the first place, not just going with the flow.'

Isabella sighed, looked down, then up at me and held my hand from across the table and said, *'I don't want to be negative Michael, but it's just all talk again, about how our situation will get better but it never does. How long are you going to carry on like this kidding yourself and your family? It can't carry on like this much longer, can it?.'*

'I totally agree with you Isabella, I have made a lot of promises in the past, but this is different. I just know it, but I also know I can't do it without your support. Please, Isabella, I'm begging you, just one more time? Let me explain a few things. You see the job you do equals the money you make and the money you make equals the lifestyle you live.'

JOB YOU DO = MONEY YOU MAKE = LIFESTYLE YOU LIVE

Work out your lifestyle, and that will guide you as to what job(s) you need to do

'The problem is our lifestyle is too high for the money we make, so how do we change it when we – or should I say I – have got us into this mess? We panic, borrow more money if we can, we worry and dig ourselves deeper and deeper, so we take it out on each other and spend the rest of our time trying to get out of the situation we got ourselves into in the first place.'

'Yes, admittedly, we got ourselves into this mess,' Isabella said.

'How do we get ourselves out of this mess?' I said,

'I don't know Michael, we could borrow some money from my parents? They offered to help while I was with them.'

'That's great Isabella, but all we are going to do is get into more debt. All we're doing is transferring our debts and not getting rid of them. It**'s our habits that got us into debt in the first place. It's not just about paying the debt, it's about us changing our habits and how we see the world, how we see money, values etc. how we do things or we will end up right back where we started**. It's our habits and beliefs that have got us into this mess in the first place. You see the Ten Steps have taught me to accept responsibility for where we are today. The first step is about accepting who you are and where you are today. Turning today into the beginning of the future and not the end.'

'Isabella, I know that I have let you down, and now I am asking you to believe in me again, not to mention the story about the voice. You are probably thinking that I am losing the plot. All I am asking of you is to read and listen to what the Ten Steps are about; the source is a separate issue. It is just like saying, I'm not going to drive a car until I understand how the combustion of an engine works, the gears, drive, shaft etc. What we need to know is whether the car is able to work? Well, the Ten Steps work, we can address the source later, but you will see that once you grasp the Ten Steps, you will be more accepting of the source.

'You probably think that out of all the people out there why did the voice pick me? Well, I don't know, maybe it's because I was so desperately in need of help. We couldn't carry on much longer as we were, could we Isabella?'

'No,' she replied.

'Isabella, please just trust me this last time. It's not just about us borrowing money, it's about us sorting our heads and lives out. It's about eliminating that negative imposter which was pulling us apart and becoming one, together again, like we were. You remember how happy we were and the dreams we shared. Do you remember Isabella?'

Isabella smiled up at me and said *'Well, Michael, you do sound different...'*

'Can I just quickly explain the Ten Steps to you?'

Isabella paused for a few seconds... *'Go on then, only because I love you.'*

'Fantastic. You won't regret this!'

It was two o'clock in the morning. We had been discussing the Ten Steps for five hours and we were both tired.

'Good job it is Sunday tomorrow, we can have a lie-in.'

'Isabella can you see why I am so excited about our future?'

'Yes I can, so long as you put it into practice. I don't know where you got these Ten Steps from, but they do make a lot of sense and are very enlightening. You do see the world from a different perspective.'

'What I need you to do Isabella, is to do your own set of goals, so that we can synchronise them together. Oh! By the way you remember I said I was having a group meeting with Ade, Lian, Brianna and Matt – you know Matt, from down the pub, always playing pool and moaning about life.'

'Oh yes, him.'

'Well I've got a meeting scheduled for tomorrow evening at Matt's place, is that okay with you? If not I'll change it. We have been taking it in turns: It would be great if you could join me and sit in on the rest of the Ten Steps. I'll ring Sofie tomorrow and ask if she would be able to watch the boys for a few hours if you would like to come'

I looked straight into Isabella's eyes… 'Isabella, thank you for being understanding and for being a wonderful wife and standing by me all this time. I believe this is our second beginning. I love you.'

'I love you too… And, Michael, I understand, it's like someone has taken a great weight off my shoulders. I feel I have been living in the past for far too long now and I'm looking forward to our future together. There's a lot of work that has to be done, but with the Ten Steps, Michael, I actually think that we can do this.'

'You know Isabella, some people live their lives in the past, some live in the future and some live for today. Life to me is learning from the past, using that to create a happier and better future.' We talked for an hour and then headed to bed.

That night we connected and made passionate love. It was just like when we had first met. What had happened to us, our relationship? The stress of modern-day living, working and bringing up Emilio and Jason had just got in the way of what was once a great relationship. Could we get back to that point in our lives again and then it happened… this was becoming a more regular occurrence, catching myself from looking back and focusing on a new beginning, that inner peace to me… Don't look back to the past, look to the future, use where you are today as a beginning and design your future the way that you want, then get a plan together.

The Ten Steps were becoming a part of my thinking process, I was evolving and that's what life is about. It's about evolving, but we must all take control of what and who we evolve into. If you're not in control of your life then someone else is. Who is in control of your life? Who? I am! And on that note, I drifted off to sleep.

The next morning I woke early. I looked at the alarm clock. It was 6.35 am. I just lay there and reflected on my life so far, the highs and the many lows. I realised that I had only been in control of my life 20% of the time, but that was the past. I am in control now. I now understand that if you control

50% or more in your life you can then begin to influence the outcome. Wow, **my life is like running a business**. First, it's a small one-man-band type of business and you are fully in control, then you get a partner and it's a 50/50 split. Then the children arrive on the scene and the split can change in your favour or out of your favour. The challenge is working on it and not giving in. 'I like that analogy,' I said to myself.

The more I think, the more I see, the more I see, the more I understand, the more I understand the more I realise how powerful and special we really are. We are like an untapped field with fantastic resources, yet most people go to their graves without ever being discovered, without their sweetest music ever being played. That's not going to happen to me, NO NOT ME. I have got a lot to give and a lot to do. I feel like Arnold Schwarzenegger in *The Terminator*. 'I'll be back!' Yes, yes, yes let the show begin, I am unstoppable now.

At this moment I jumped out of my bed, punched the air and said 'I feel great and I am unstoppable.' Isabella woke up startled.

'What's going on? Is everything okay?'

I had forgotten Isabella was still in bed. 'Yes,' I replied as I leaned over and gave her a hug and a kiss. 'I just feel great. I just feel so happy and last night was just amazing.'

'If you feel that good, why don't you get back into bed?' Isabella said with a smile on her face. I realised that this was a real opportunity not to be refused and got back into bed…

CHAPTER SEVEN

Step Six: Take all your goals and make a Plan of Action

Isabella and I fell asleep in each other's arms, snuggled up all cosy. I stirred and looked at the alarm clock. It was now 8:30 am on Sunday morning. The sunlight was peeping through a gap in the curtains. I looked at Isabella and she was still sleeping, so I carefully got out of bed so as not to disturb her. I went into the boys' room and woke them. We all went downstairs and had some breakfast. As I was eating my toast, I reflected on last night and smiled. I was so happy that Isabella had taken on board what I had told her about the Ten Steps. Heck, she was even embracing them! I dressed the boys and we went to church. I had to say a big thank you.

We got back about 12.30 only to find Isabella in the kitchen going through the Ten Steps. *'Michael,'* she said as I walked in, *'these Ten Steps are amazing. I got up not long after you left and couldn't help but think about the Ten Steps. So I got them out and started reading and I haven't been able to put them down.'*

Well, I just stood back in amazement; I never expected this reaction from Isabella.

'Michael, I know you will understand, but can you look after Emilio and Jason today, I would really like to spend some time on the Ten Steps myself. You know that bit where we have time for all the trivial things in our lives, but not the important things and I'd like to spend my time today on the Ten Steps, not washing, cleaning or ironing. Is that okay?'

Well, I was lost for words, 'Yes, yes,' I said. '... the only problem is we are meeting at Matt's tonight.'

'Ah… the babysitter rang whilst you were out. Something has come up and she can't look after the boys for us this evening, so you will have to go to the meeting by yourself.'

'That's a shame, but I'll give you any help you need and oh, I forgot we are supposed to be holding the next meeting here on Monday evening is that okay?'

'Yes, that's great,' said Isabella.

I couldn't believe my ears. 'Well I'll take the boys out for the day, grab a spot of lunch and leave you to it' and with that, the boys and I got into the car and started chatting about the day we were going to have together.

We had a great day. We went to the local garden centre, which had a giant play area. Then we had lunch and went swimming. I had missed Jason and Emilio this last week. In fact, I had been so caught up in the stresses of our situation I hadn't been there for them very often at all. I was always busy doing something or worrying about something.

One of the failings that we have as humans is that we get so wrapped up in being busy, we lose track of what is happening around us in our day-to-day family lives. We get caught up in our own world; we forget there is a world out there to explore. My problem, or should I say challenge, is that I wanted a great family life and a career too. Were these two things possible together?

Well, anything is possible if we work hard enough at it. I knew though, that without Isabella's support, it would not be possible, or it would make it very difficult.

We got back at five o'clock; Isabella was still engrossed in the Ten Steps, so I cooked dinner. It had been a long time since Isabella and I were in harmony together. It just goes to show how powerful these Ten Steps are when you apply them.

We had a lovely family dinner together then I got ready to go to Matt's and Isabella carried on with the Ten Steps. *'Michael, I can see why you have been so engrossed and committed to the Ten Steps. Once you start you can't stop.'*

We said our goodbyes; I gave Isabella a big hug and a kiss and the boys too. It was a brilliant feeling that we were a loving, caring family again.

I was the first to arrive at Matt's place and witnessed the beginning of the new Matt.

'Good evening, Michael,' he said. *'I'm glad you are the first here. I want to ask a favour of you, if you don't mind.'*

'Well yes, but it does depend on what,' I said, looking quite suspicious.

'What I would like you to do is whenever you see me straying from my goals, slacking, falling back into my bad habits please tell me. I feel like a ship lost at sea with no rudder and the coast guard that's you, has just found me. I want to thank you and let you know that I will not let you down, but please keep an eye on me.'

'Well Matt, thanks for those kind words. I feel privileged to be an instrument of delivery for the Ten Steps but as the Ten Steps state, you have to be at a certain point in your life, to one receive them, and to act on it. The key though Matt, is to pass it on, so when we are finished and you feel confident, you need to pass the Ten Steps on because the more people you help in life, the more humble, content and confident you are with yourself; and the more you like yourself.'

Just then the doorbell rang, it was the others.

'Wow!' said Brianna to Matt, *'You look great, what have you done to yourself.'*

Matt was shy and put his head down and muttered, *'It's the new me. I decided to take more pride in how I look.'* I hadn't noticed but Matt had shaved, put on a crisp white shirt and a blue tie patterned with daisies – and he had also tidied up his flat and lit scented candles.

'Well Matt, you look great,' we all said.

We all settled down. 'Just before we start I want to let you all know that Isabella came home from her parents' house in Spain and she has started reading up on the Ten Steps. She is also very excited about them and how we can go about changing our lives. She was going to join us this evening, but the babysitter cancelled, so she will sit in with us on our next meeting as were having it at our place.'

Everyone was happy that Isabella would be on board and part of our group.

I went on. 'The process of change has begun. We are all different people from how we were seven days ago, our outlooks are different, but we can't maintain this transformation unless we stay focused and committed. This is the easy part, while we meet up every day in a group. How will you be able to sustain working on your plans on your own?

'Step Six is about taking all your goals and making a plan of action. There are five simple steps to take. I apologise for repeating myself but have you heard of the saying that 'people don't plan to fail, they just fail to plan.' A goal without a plan to action is a wish, a dream. That's like having a goal to play the guitar but not buying a guitar or taking guitar lessons. It's not really a goal is it? So, what I'd like is for everyone to share some of your goals with us and I'll explain how this exercise works'

Ade and Lian were the first to speak, *'We want a bigger house but we just can't afford it at the moment.'*

'Thanks for that, but you can see what you've just done, you have a goal, but in the same breath, you have unconsciously said it's not going to happen. I'll explain more in a moment. Brianna what goal are you going to share with us?'

'Well, I feel a little shy saying this, but I want to be promoted to head of my department at work. I believe I can do a better job than Tom.'

'Well that's intriguing,' said Ade.

'Matt, what goal are you going to share with us?'

'The last few days have really made me think about my life and my goal is not to waste any more time, to try and do something with it. The problem is I don't know what.'

'Thank you for sharing those goals with us.'

'How about you Michael?' asked Matt, *'Are you going to share one of your goals with us?'*

'Well, yes.' I replied. 'I wasn't expecting to, but I should contribute one to the group. Let me see, I know what, my main goal is to make £50,000 a year and to spend more quality time with my family. So there you have it… let's get started'

'First let's look at our goals, as I just mentioned – mine is to increase my annual income by £30,000 up to £50,000 a year and while doing this, I want to spend more quality time with my family. So, I want more money but I want to work less. Interesting isn't it?

'You see our first step in goal setting is to clearly establish what do you really want, then the second step is how important is the goal to you? I mean how badly do you want it? What commitments or sacrifices are you prepared to make to meet your goals? **If you are not committed to a goal or prepared to make sacrifices for the goal, you cannot achieve it.**

'What I'm going to do is go through my goal quickly and then go through yours individually. Then we can all do the exercise later. Your future is worth investing some time and thought into, isn't it? So much has happened in the last five days, I haven't had time, especially with our meetings to fully work on mine, but here it is.'

'Don't forget, no excuses Michael,' Matt said jokingly.

We all giggled.

The five steps are:

Number One: Articulate the goal. What I mean by this is to put it into words

My goal is to earn £50,000+ per annum and to spend more quality time with my family.

Number Two: Establish why is it important to you

'One of the most important things you need to do when you look at your goal list is to choose a big enough goal that when you achieve it, it takes care of a lot of little goals. So, for example, my goal of £50,000 takes care of the house Isabella and I want, the car, the holidays, the clothes, most of the material things we desire. It will eliminate the financial-related stress on the family and we will have more quality time to enjoy ourselves together as a family. The first thing your inner voice says to you is to forget it, that's an impossible task; it's too hard, you've never done anything like that before, why start now?

This is the old you talking. It's important as you move forward that when you have this inner dialogue with yourself that you know whether it is the old you or the new you talking.

'The only way you can fight that negative talk is with a plan backed by commitment and actions. When we focus on why our goal is important to us; we can fight off those negative thoughts because the alternative is to stay where we are. **Do you want to spend the rest of your life the way it is now? Or do you want to change it for a better and more fulfilling life?**

'I definitely don't want to stay the same,' said Matt, *'I'm sick and tired of being sick and tired. I want to do something with my life, I just don't know what.'*

'I'll come to that in a moment,' I replied.

Number Three: Set a deadline.

'Decide when you want to achieve this by. For example, I have set a date of two years from now, but achieving this goal in one year would be better.'

Number Four: What skills do I need to acquire or develop to achieve my goal? What one skill, if I excelled in it, would help me achieve my goal?

Number Five: How are you going to achieve your goal? What's your plan of action?

'How can I increase my income from £20,000 to £50,000? First, what we have to do is make a list of options. This is the list that I have come up with so far:

a)   Earn a promotion at work; this could only account for £10,000 of the £50,000.

b)   Enrol and attend a range of courses such as night classes to enhance my qualifications. But before I do that, I need to know what the financial impact will be. I see a lot of people who do night classes and extra courses but they still fail to gain any kind of promotion. It looks good on paper but not in your pay packet. There are so many courses now, at university that when you graduate, you can't even get a job with your qualification. So, you either have to complete an additional, supplementary course or try something new. It's amazing how many people go to university or to night classes without performing enough research to see how the course they're doing is going to benefit them financially. It's just like the I.T. business, you can complete a course in one area of computing and the pay is low and you can complete one course in another area, but the pay is high. They are both I.T. related courses, but one is more prosperous than the other… the pay range is vast.

c)   My next option is to change career, maybe into sales, start a business, or buy a franchise. That's a big step and may require the appropriate research and funding.

d)   Conduct some business alongside work, e.g., buying and selling, the internet or part-time sales. In fact, a great way to make an extra income and grow is direct sales, build it up then when it's going well, take it on full time. There are so many success stories out there of how people have worked hard and grown.

'I need to look at what side hustle, direct sales, courses, businesses, and jobs that I can do that will give me what I want in terms of financial return and satisfaction. I've then got to establish which one of these jobs I want to do but it must have the potential to deliver my goal. Work out how long it is going to take to get it into place etc. to see if it will fall within my time plan of two years for example.'

e)   The last option is to do nothing, maybe say a prayer and hope. This reminds me of another story of a man who prayed every day for thirty years to God to win the lottery, all he wanted was £1 million. Thirty years on, he dies and he goes to heaven. He sees St. Peter at the pearly gates of heaven, "Where is God?" he asks, ""Why?" said St. Peter. "I want to have a word with him, because he let me down." "He is busy at the moment," said St. Peter; "Can I help?" "I just don't understand, for thirty years I prayed every day to God to help me win the lottery and nothing ever happened. I'm a good Christian. I thought for the first few years, he was busy and would eventually get around to me, but for thirty years no response." "Ah," said St. Peter, "we have been discussing you for the last ten years, I know about your case. The problem that God had was you never bought a lottery ticket. How can we help you win, when you weren't even in the lottery in the first place? Just like the lottery saying; you have to be in it, to win it!"

'You can't win the race if you are not in the race. Your goals can't happen without taking action. Right guys, that's what you have to do with your goals.'

'This is hard work,' Matt said.

'I know it sounds like hard work, but once you get into it, you get used to it. Think of it as a pool or snooker game. It's your turn, you know what you have to do to win the game, and you have a plan, now you need the skill to execute your plan. One step at a time, always playing the white ball ready for the next shot. That's goal setting with a plan of action.'

'I get it,' said Matt.

'The importance of this exercise lies in how significant is the goal to you or how badly do you want it. If you don't want it bad enough then you are not ready for change and you lose your focus. Your goals just become a wish. I know that we keep coming back to this point but you do have to be at a crossroads, a point in your life where you are ready to embrace the Ten Steps.'

Go to exercises for Chapter 7

'Remember one of the conditions the voice gave us at the beginning. Once you begin the Ten Steps, you must commit to the full programme.

'Is spending a few hours designing your next twenty, thirty, forty, fifty-plus years of your life, worth it or not? Only you can decide. What I want you all to do now is close your eyes and answer this question to yourself and not to me. **Is it worth it to you, to commit to these steps and to invest a few hours of your time to design the next thirty, forty, fifty-plus years of your life?** Is it worth it, yes or no?...'

With that, I closed my eyes and said nothing for one minute. I used this time to reaffirm my commitment to the Ten Steps. I could only assume the others did the same...

'Time is up, and as I said, keep your answer to yourself. You're not doing this for me; you're doing it for yourself and your family.'

'Now, regardless of how you feel you must complete the Ten Steps, but your level of commitment will be directly related to how you feel. Let's take one minute to close our eyes and make a choice about the life we want or to keep the life we have now? The choice is yours' Again I closed my eyes first. 'If you feel like writing your answer down, please do.'

One minute felt like ten minutes. 'Okay your time is up. Keep your decision to yourself. What I am going to do now is go through your goals quickly and then we will finish for the night.' It was twelve minutes after ten.

'I can't believe just how quick the time seems to fly,' said Ade.

'Right, Ade and Lian, your goal is to get a bigger house. Why is this goal important to you?'

Lian replied first. *'Well we have two kids and live in a two-bedroom house. We want a four-bedroom house and a big garden, because I love gardening. I've always wanted my own garden so that I can grow my own vegetables. We want our children to have their own individual bedrooms. We always said that when we had kids they would not have to share a bedroom.'*

'I want one for an office,' said Ade. *'I need it for my Zoom calls and sales business I want to do.'*

'Great, Ade and Lian, I can see you have put some thought into it.'

'Ok so we have the goal written down and review why it's important to you.

'You first need to describe in more detail, the better the detail the easier it is to achieve e.g., what type of four-bedroom house you want? Is it detached, is it a townhouse? What sort of kitchen, bedrooms, and garage do you want etc.? Do you want a new house, old house or cottage? What part of town do you want to live in? How big do you want the garden, how large do you want the garage? There are lots of elements to take into consideration and from all those factors; we can then determine the rough price guide of the house.

'Have you thought about all those factors?'

'Not all of them but most of them. We want a cottage on the outskirts of town. I love the countryside but we don't want it to be too far away from schools etc. The price would be about £300,000.'

'Sounds like a nice house,' Brianna said,

'It should be for £300,000,' Matt exclaimed in a jovial way.

'No wise remarks please, Lian and Ade have been good to share their goal with us and we are not to comment. This is a good example because most people want a nice house.'

'The next stage is to set a deadline. When would you like to have your house by?'

'It would be nice to have a house like that in five to ten years.'

'Listen to the words you're using. It would be nice; there is no commitment or belief in it and the five to ten years is unspecific and too long. How badly do you want this goal? Five to ten years is too vague, sounds like a wish. If your goal is too far away you are going to struggle with the commitment to stay the course. Most people are too afraid to set deadlines because they believe if they don't achieve their goal by that date they have failed. Remember you only fail when you…'

'Quit,' everyone replied.

'You see if you set a deadline for say, two years for your new home, what that does is provide a pace of urgency. Now if it takes three years instead of two years, fantastic, but I don't believe you will have achieved it in three years if you set a goal of five to ten years. Can you see that?'

'Yes I am beginning to understand how this works, the deadline you set is what brings the goals to life with urgency,' said Ade

'The next thing I'm going to say is very important. There are no wrong goals, only wrong time lines. What do I mean? You set a goal to achieve by your birthday two years from now if you don't hit the goal you don't give up on the goal just adjust the timeline… does that make sense?'

'You know, I used to set goals and when I didn't achieve them by the timeline I set, I gave up and then stopped setting goals,' said Matt. *'Now I understand it was the wrong thing to do to give up on my goal.'*

'So, shall we start again?' I said. 'Two years for your new home?'

'Yes,' said Lian, *'That sounds exciting.'*

'I'm glad that you said that Lian, goals need to be exciting or why chase after them? Now the next step is the fun part, how do we achieve this? We now know what type of house, how much it will cost and in what area you want to live in. Are you following me so far?'

'Yes,' said everyone.

'It's exciting, isn't it?' I said. 'The next step is to work out a plan on how much the mortgage payments are, what type of mortgage do you want? It's worth speaking to a mortgage broker to explain all the different types of mortgages and which would be more suitable to your circumstances. Most people say they cannot afford it and give up when they don't even know what the costs are and what options are available. Now you have mortgage payments, you then need to work out your finances to see if you can afford it. If you can't, you can work out what the shortfall is; don't forget to work out the running costs of the house too, this can cause problems later. Now you know what your shortfall is in relation to your income. Therefore, the backup plan should include how you intend to increase your income and credit rating? Can you see by applying these simple principles you can increase your chance of achieving your goals by 100%, 200% or more. And don't forget what skill level you would need to pull all of this off.'

'I remember once when I was listening to some podcasts by a great motivational speaker Brian Tracy, where he talked about a study conducted at Harvard University on graduates leaving. What they found was that only 3% to 4% of the graduates had clearly defined goals. I think it was about ten or twenty years later, the 3% of graduates with goals were worth more than the remaining 97% put together.'

'You make it sound so easy,' said Ade.

'It's not easy, it's just a simple step by step process that we should be taught from ten or eleven years old and it can change your life. Lian and Ade, now you know what to do.'

'Thanks Michael, we will put it into practice.'

'I am glad you said that because that's the catch if you were looking for one… **putting it into action**.'

'Brianna, your goal is to get promoted to head of your department, isn't it?'

'Yes it is. I understand the process now; I think I can do it myself.'

'Great, there's only one thing to watch out for. You might want to head the department but is there a vacancy for you to apply for? You might have to consider moving to another company. Make sure your plan does not mean you have to wait around for someone to leave or get the sack, because then you lose control of your goal. Minimise the people you need to depend on, it gives you more control and less excuses for not achieving your goal. Do you all understand that?'

'Yes,' replied everyone.

In fact, it might be worth speaking to your boss about your desire to be head of a department, and to ask them to advise you what you need to do to get that position and in what time frame. Then you know what skill level you need to acquire and then you can make a plan.

'Now Matt, your goal is not to waste anymore of your life, to do something with it, the only problem is you don't know what.'

'Yes, it's just since my divorce, losing everything, I can't see the point of working, making money and giving it to my ex and debtors, not to mention paying tax as well, can you?'

'How old is your daughter?'

'She is six.'

'Now you can't sit on your backside for the next ten years. Have you got ten years to waste?'

'No, I haven't.'

'Well, just accept these outgoings as your overheads that you have to pay. Do you love your daughter?'

'Yes, I do,' Matt said strongly.

'Do you want her to remember you as a failure or someone who took control of his life?' There was a pause for a few seconds.

'Someone who took control.'

'Now we have the reason why your goal is important to you. You don't want to let yourself and your daughter down, do you?'

'No I don't, I've let her down enough; I need to change now, yes now.'

'Good for you. How much money would you like to make? Don't forget the formula that you need to do: **the job you do equals the money you make, which equals the lifestyle you have**. So determine your lifestyle which then determines the money you need to make and that determines the job or jobs you need to do.

THE JOB YOU DO = THE MONEY YOU MAKE = THE LIFESTYLE YOU LIVE
OR
THE LIFESTYLE YOU WANT = THE MONEY YOU NEED TO MAKE = THE JOB(S) YOU NEED TO DO

'I know, but I am not money-oriented. I wouldn't say I was a very materialistic person. That's why I got myself into so much of a mess.'

'It's not about money Matt, it's about the lifestyle you want to have or the person you want to be. You can't expect heat, and not be prepared to make a fire.

'Making and managing money is not the same as being materialistic. Whether you are materialistic or not, you need money to live in the Western world. So we do need a certain amount of money. There's nothing wrong in making more money than you need and giving to charities from your excess. First let's set a deadline to begin your re-entry into the modern world, the rat race, the game of life whatever you want to call it. I suggest three to six months, we need to take action now'

'*Three to six months!*' said Matt.

'Yes three to six months. If ever you're going to do it, it has to be now. Now or never. Stop and think of your daughter. Do you want her to be ashamed of you or proud of you, which one?'

The room was quiet and everyone's gaze focused on Matt.

'*I feel like I am being pressured here,*' said Matt.

'There's no pressure, you are the one putting yourself under pressure because you won't commit to your decision. To do nothing and to procras- tinate is to choose failure. Success or failure? The choice is yours. If you don't take action, you have to decide to accept your situation. Matt there are times in life where you are going to have to trust someone or trust your gut instinct. You can't let your fears, uncertainties and doubts control you, can you now?'

'*No, I can't, I'm just scared.*'

'There's nothing wrong in being scared' I said in a soft voice. 'We're all scared, it's just some of us handle it better than others.'

'You are probably sick of my sayings, but here is another one. "A hero dies once when he faces his fears but a coward dies a thousand deaths." Remember in one of our earlier sessions, when I said imagine you're at your own funeral, how would you like to be remembered?'

'*I remember that,*' Matt said. '*That's one of the parts that woke me up.*'

'Look Matt, as I said earlier the timescale of the goal only gives you a focus point to work towards. There's no jury going to try you in six months from now. But the fact is you can actually do it in less time.'

'*Okay, Michael,*' Matt said, '*I know that you are right. Six months it is. I'm committed.*'

Everyone cheered Matt.

'It's getting late,' Lian said.

Matt shuffled in his chair, looked at his feet and mumbled 'I know I'm so sorry, it's all my fault, isn't it?'

'Will you stop blaming yourself?' Lian intervened. *'I was only making the remark as we all have to work tomorrow, it wasn't aimed at you. I'm sorry.'*

'It's important I finish this last section for Matt. So, if any of you want to go, that's fine. Matt and I can carry on for as long as we need to.

Ade and Lian stood up and said they needed to go, *'We know what to do now, take our goals, find out why it's important to us to achieve it. Set a deadline to achieve it, establish what skills we need to develop or acquire to achieve our goal and make a plan of action on how to achieve it. And don't forget the skills we need to develop or acquire to achieve our goals. Ahh, another important point — don't forget to include in our plan any potential challenges we might have and how we will overcome them.'*

'That's right, you have got it in one' I said. 'On Sunday we will start the next step, which is an extension of this one, just to help you zero in more.'

Ade and Lian said their goodbyes and Brianna also said that she would leave so that both Matt and I could get down to the nitty-gritty of what he needed to do.

Matt told Brianna that she was more than welcome to stay and listen to the nuggets of information that Michael would have for him, so she sat back down and made herself comfortable, curling up into one of Matt's large armchairs.

Matt and I continued. 'The next step, Matt, is to make a plan of how you can achieve this goal. Firstly, because you haven't got a specific idea of what you want to do, we need to find one we can focus on. So, what we need to do is make a list of all the things you like doing. For example, you like playing pool and snooker. What else do you like doing?'

'I love playing on my PlayStation, surfing the internet and I like drinking.'

'Now, seriously Matt, are there any jobs you have ever done and got enjoyment from?'

'Well, yes I used to be an electrician before I got the sack. I had too much time off work with the divorce. I couldn't concentrate on my work and one day someone nearly got electrocuted because I didn't check the wiring properly. They were ok, but it could have been much worse – what if I had killed them…? I didn't follow the procedure, so I got the sack.'

'Did you enjoy your job?'

'Yes I did actually. I enjoyed solving the problems when there was a fault.'

'That's very good Matt, what else did you enjoy doing?'

'Well I used to do a lot of jobs for people outside of work. I enjoyed being popular and people wanting my services.'

'Did you now?' said Brianna with a humorous tone.

'Seriously, it made me feel great, the only problem was that I was never at home. I was always off working, helping someone and I didn't charge the right amount so my wife wasn't very happy.' Matt paused for a second and his head dropped as his face went from happy to sad. *'That's why I lost my wife. I was never home and didn't have much to show for it. As I said I am not a very good businessman. I let people use me and it cost me my family.'*

'You know Matt; I used to think of you as a bit of a loser. Someone who couldn't be bothered. But I do understand you more now. I have seen a different side of you and an understanding of why you act the way that you have in the past,' said Brianna.

'We're all born to win, but you must see it to achieve. It is easy to put people down, to judge them before you have considered their side of the story and get the full facts. I've always liked that passage in the Bible where it says **'He**

who is without sin cast the first stone.' We're not perfect, our experiences have brought us to this point in life, good or bad but we must accept that what we are today is as a result of our choices. Conscious or unconscious that we have made and so long as you see where you are today as the beginning, the future is always bright.'

'Matt, can I ask you a question?'

'Yes, Michael, you can.'

'Are you serious about doing something with your life? Are you prepared to start changing now, make the decisions now, to go forward, to look to the future and not the past? Are you ready? Before you answer Matt, please just have a think about it, get it clear in your mind. I'm just going to excuse myself for a few moments as I need to message Isabella and let her know I'll be home a little later than I'd anticipated. It's all good though, I'm happy to stay with you until we have sussed out what needs to be done to help you. Brianna, do you mind stepping into the kitchen so Matt can think please?'

I came back, called Brianna into the room 'Right, Matt, are you ready?'

'Yes I am, I can't explain how I feel, I just know that what we are doing is right. I know I'm weak and lack confidence.'

'Here we go again, stop doing that!' said Brianna.

'This time just hear me out,' said Matt. *'I feel like an onion being peeled and every day we seem to be taking another layer off. I've spent all day today, looking forward to our meeting. I also want to thank you all for your support. I know I've been a miserable person for a while, I know I couldn't have gotten this far without your support and one day I'm going to pay you all back.'*

'The only payment we want from you Matt is to start believing in yourself that you can change. One of the requirements of the Ten Steps is to reach out and touch someone else. We all need help and support and I shall be covering that point the next time that we meet up, but I can tell that you do want to change. One of the greatest gifts we have is to care and love for one another and one of the greatest satisfactions we get is when that love and care is acknowledged and reciprocated!'

I looked Matt in the eyes, 'Matt you are a special person with lots of good qualities. **You have got what it takes and we believe in you. All you need to do is believe in yourself, WHY NOT YOU! Why shouldn't you deserve a chance, why not you!** We get knock downs in life, but the true crime is staying down – get up!'

'So, coming back to your goal, what we need to do is recap and find a job goal that you like that will give you what you want. We know what you are good at and we know you want your daughter to be proud of you. So can I suggest that in your case, what you need is two goals? One is to break your current situation; to get out of the rut you are in, and the other to do something that will make your daughter proud of you. You need to go back to your original list of goals that we completed in Step Three, conduct some research and find a job. That will firstly get you out of the rut and secondly a job that is in harmony with your long-term goals. For example, you can get a job as an electrician again, with the intention to set up your own electrical business with people working for you to enable you to have time off for you to spend some time with your daughter or maybe do some charitable work. This could involve working for a charitable housing association. Kill two birds with one stone.

'I hate to bring the issue of money up again, but your income determines your lifestyle. So give yourself a chance. Money is like alcohol; to some people it brings out the good, loving and fun person you are and to others it brings out the worst in them. Unfortunately, we only hear about the bad examples of people who use money in a ruthless or unethical manner, and we very rarely hear about the good examples of people who use money in a giving or philanthropic way. Which one are you?'

'The good, I suppose,' said Matt.

'There is no harm in making money so long as you make it honestly and ethically. Unfortunately it is difficult to survive in the modern world we live in today, without money. So make sure your plan includes making a certain amount of money.

'Money is a by-product of successful work habits!

'So, Matt, to recap, **firstly set your goals, make sure it's a goal you really desire, then secondly establish why this is important to you. Thirdly, set a deadline to achieve it by, for example, you can find employment in three weeks, but we said three to six months, just focus on it. Fourthly, determine the skills you need to obtain to achieve your goal. Identify the obstacles you would need to overcome to achieve your goal. Lastly, make a plan of action on how to achieve it**. Have you got that Matt?'

'Yes I have, the ball is in my court, and it's up to me to figure out what I'm going to do and why I am going to do it… You forget one step Michael… Believe in yourself'

'That's right Matt. I can tell you what to do, but when it's your idea and you believe in yourself, it has a better chance of being successful,' I said.

'I'm not going to let you down, Michael. But more importantly, I feel I am not going to let myself or my daughter down. I understand that I have to take full responsibility for my future, and you know what?… I'm going to do exactly that! I feel fired up, I feel ready. Thank you Michael for sharing these Ten Steps with me. I'm starting to feel like a different man already, just by taking this time this evening and working out what I need to do. It's like a shining beacon of light glowing at the end of a tunnel of hope.'

I smiled at Matt. I believed that he would achieve his goals. He had a certain air about himself this evening that had positivity bubbling through.

Brianna and I left Matt's place, and I walked her to her car. *'Thank you for tonight, Michael. Matt was really glowing wasn't he! Bless him, I think he's found his mojo all thanks to you.'*

'Thanks, Brianna. Good night. Drive safely.' And with that I walked to my car, which incidentally was only parked two cars away from Brianna's, and drove the short distance home. I felt especially tired tonight, and I was looking forward to cuddling up to Isabella when I got in.

CHAPTER EIGHT

Step Seven: Establish your Quitability Point — NEVER, NEVER QUIT

I woke early on Monday. The sun was shining, the birds were singing, and Isabella was sleeping peacefully at the side of me. I stroked her chestnut hair that was spilling over her pillow. She looked beautiful. My heart leapt with love. I was so thankful that Isabella was on board and supported the Ten Steps. I just knew that we would make it, and our lives were going to turn around and be so much better from now on.

When I arrived at the office, I was buzzing. Everybody noticed, but only Ade and Brianna understood why.

Well, not all of it… I smiled.

I felt good because things were beginning to take shape. The journey had begun, and I was positive.

The day went by in a blur. I couldn't help but think that we were coming near to the end of the Ten Steps program. We were getting used to meeting up every night, but we were all going to have to start to work through the Ten Steps of our own volition. We all had goals, and each one of us had something different that we needed to – and would – achieve.

I thought for a moment and decided that we should discuss this, and maybe we have a get together once a month to catch up and be a sounding board for each other.

I got home at 5:30 pm, the table was laid, a glass of red wine poured out, and the food smelled beautiful. It was my favourite: salmon with lemon, garlic rice and vegetables. Isabella walked into the dining room holding a glass of wine, and she looked happy. I gave her a big hug and a kiss and complimented her on the meal. We sat down and had a lovely dinner together.

I was still trying to get the boys off to bed when the doorbell rang. It was Ade and Lian. They hadn't seen Isabella for a few weeks, so I knew they would be catching up on the latest gossip.

When I came down, Matt and Brianna had arrived. They were talking about the Ten Steps. Ade and Lian remarked that they had never seen Isabella so radiant before and how well she looked.

'I know she's beautiful isn't she?' I said and stared into her eyes.

'I thought this was a training session on the Ten Steps, not a love scene, look at you two,' said Brianna with a smile and a wink.

'It's amazing what the Ten Steps can do for you, when you share it with the one you love.' I said. 'Anyway shall we get down to it? *Err, pardon the expression.'* Everyone laughed.

'Before we start on Step Seven, how did we all do with our exercises on Step Five and Six?'

Brianna was the first to speak; *'I'm just finding it difficult to find the time to do the exercises between working, housework and our meetings. There just doesn't seem to be any time and by the time I get home I am tired.'*

'I'm the opposite,' said Matt. *'When I get home, I am buzzing and can't sleep.'*

Yes, but you don't have to go to work in the morning,' Brianna replied in a sarcastic tone.

'Okay, let's not get personal; this is what we are going to do. We will spend the next hour reviewing and catching up on all of our exercises. It's important that we're all up to date before going to the next step. The key to doing your exercises is to be honest with yourself; nobody will see what you put down, only you. I suggest we go into separate rooms, so there are no distractions. *Isabella and I will go upstairs.'*

'Now behave yourselves,' said Ade in a joking manner.

'Can I use the kitchen?' Brianna said.

'Yes, you can. Matt can use the dining room, and Ade and Lian can use the sitting room.'

I was grateful for the time. Brianna was right. It had been a hectic few days and I needed some time to reflect on my exercises. I knew I had changed in the last week, and it was an opportunity for Isabella and me to review our goals together. We all set off to do our exercises. Just then, I remembered a saying my mother always used to say to me; 'Don't put off what you can do today till tomorrow.'

I set the timer on my phone to go off in an hour. It went by so quickly, we all gathered back together in the living room.

'Right, how are we doing?'

Ade was the first to speak, *'There is a side to me, I've been suppressing, a side I don't want to acknowledge and there's also a side to me I don't want to see but I am afraid to show it. I suppose I haven't got the confidence,'* said Ade.

'That's a very good point,' I said. 'It is frightening to look into our inner selves and review, understand and analyse, who we are and how we got to this point in our lives today.

Remember your beliefs today, right or wrong, control you, so if you don't look at your past, you don't know who your boss is and who is controlling you. Does that make sense?'

'Yes I think I get it,' said Ade.

'The question is, will your beliefs empower you or dis-empower you? Can you see why it's important to constantly review and revisit these exercises, because the more you look and think about these, the more you see – not to mention as you develop and grow – your perspective changes and your new beliefs mean you look at everything differently. Once again, our life is an endless journey of evolving. **Don't stop the evolution, control it.** Right the next step, following on and this is very important...

'**Step Seven** is about establishing before you start to work on your goals, what is your quitability point. At what point do you give up on your goals? You see, it's important that you are very clear about what your goals are and what you want out of your life so that when you commit to them there's no going back, no quitting when the going gets tough. It's like saying "When the going gets tough, the tough get going." Tough times don't last, but tough people do... you see toughness is about not giving up – don't be a quitter. Another saying, "It's not how big the dog is in the fight. It's how much fight there is in the dog that makes the difference."'

'You can't become a success in life if you are a quitter. It's easy to quit something that you don't realise how important it is to you. Let me ask you a question: if your child was in trouble and they needed your help, at what point would you give up on rescuing them? You wouldn't, would you? Your life and your goals are essential.

'Your success is directly related to your quitability point. **Your quitability point is the weakest link in the chain.** You will be tested, it's not an easy road, there will be obstacles, days you feel really low; they but so long as you don't quit, you'll always win! The world is full of people who quit on themselves, they are full of regret because they know in their mind, if they persisted and had not given up, their lives would be different. Don't get me wrong; if you choose a goal that makes you feel ill and affects your health, it's not a good goal for you, so change it. Establishing a quitability point is like a boxer going into the ring knowing that to stand a chance of winning, he has to be prepared to go the full twelve rounds without being injured or knocked out. He trains for fifteen rounds. Is that you?

'Success takes guts, courage, commitment and belief. People die for their beliefs. Their quitability point is death. Now we are not asking you to do that, what Step Seven is all about is looking at your goals and making a very strong commitment to them. In other words you're not going to be easily discouraged. It's just like my goal of earning £50,000 a year or your goal, Ade and Lian of buying a bigger house. We decided what our goals are and now we've got a plan and we're not going to give up on the goals are we?'

'No we're not,' Ade and Lian chimed in unison. They both looked at each other and laughed. 'Well, that has confirmed the move, then!' exclaimed Ade

'We will be tempted, even Jesus was tempted, but you have to stay with your goals and beliefs. Quitability point determines how important your goals are, and price you are prepared to pay to achieve them.

'It's like buying jewellery, a house, car etc. if you really, really want it. You go to all extent and expenses to get them. Even taking out a loan with interest and repaying over a period of time.

'The point that I am trying to make is how bad you want your goals and what price you are prepared to pay to achieve them. How far will you go honestly and ethically to achieve them? How far?

'I heard of a speech that Winston Churchill gave during the Second World War. It was time for him to speak; all eyes were on him. Britain was in the thick of the war, we had our work cut out, everyone knew that when Mr. Churchill went up to the podium. He just stood there for two minutes staring at everyone then in a loud voice, he said, "NEVER GIVE IN. NEVER GIVE IN. NEVER, NEVER, NEVER, NEVER – IN NOTHING, GREAT OR SMALL, LARGE OR PETTY – NEVER GIVE IN, EXCEPT TO CONVICTIONS OF HONOUR AND GOOD SENSE…" Well, he got a standing ovation, the rest is history. Can you imagine what would have happened if Winston Churchill had given up? He used his carefully planned words, and left no doubt in anyone's mind about the outcome of the war.'

'Edmund Hillary on his first attempt to climb Mount Everest failed and nearly died of frostbite. At a banquet in recognition of his attempt, Edmund was asked to speak. Edmund looked at a picture of Mount Everest on the wall and said, "I will come again and conquer you because as a mountain you can't grow… but as a human, I can," and he went on to conquer Mount Everest. You see, the only time you fail is when you quit.

'Failure is not failure, quitting is failure.

'Another modern-day example of not giving up was Tony Bullimore, whose yacht capsized in the ocean whilst trying to compete in the Vendee Globe single-handed race. He spent four days in the upturned hull of his boat and eating chocolate bars to survive. He wouldn't just give up. He believed he would be saved. It took the Royal Navy four days to get to his boat. Everyone assumed he must be dead by now but it's a good job Bullimore didn't think that way isn't it?

'There are so many examples of how we as humans refused to give up… just like the miners stuck underground in Mexico.

'The list goes on…

Ade said, *'We are at war with our emotions and I am the Director of Flight Operations, as in Apollo 13 when the astronauts were not supposed to survive but Gene Kranz the flight director said no one has died on my watch Failure is not an option… in other words, I am the Director of my life and Failure is not an OPTION!'*

'You are beginning to sound like Michael,' Matt said, *'But I really like that analogy, I am at war with my life, thanks Ade. I really like that I am at war and I am going to win!'*

'Good for you Matt, I believe we're all beginning to get into the spirit of the Ten Steps. We might have lost a few battles but we have not lost the war. The war on you.

Think about it, we are at war with our emotions and the enemy is guilt, blame, lack of confidence, negative people, our belief system etc. We can conquer them so long as we don't give up on ourselves.

'Once you have set a goal, at the same time set a quitability point, your chances of achieving that goal will increase 100%+

'Let me give you my last example. Nelson Mandela was put in prison for years. This man suffered so many trials and tribulations. When asked the question, "How did you cope? How did you survive all those years in prison not being bitter? How do you do it?" Nelson Mandela replied in a calm voice, "My years in prison were the years that I used to prepare myself to lead my country"'

'Wow, what vision, you can see why he was a great man. Nelson knew, no! – he believed – that one day he would leave the prison and he had to be ready to lead his country then. **They can put you into prison but only you, yes only you can put your mind in prison.** We have the power, we are born successful, just tap into it with the Ten Steps and never, never, ever quit. Decide what you want and go for it.'

'I really understand what you mean,' said Matt. *'That's how I became good at playing pool and snooker. I used to get beaten, but I practised and I practised and I gained some training from a professional, until I could beat most people.'*

'Trust you to compare Mr. Nelson Mandela to playing a game of pool,' said Ade.

'We all have our own stories of where we hung in and wouldn't give up; we wouldn't quit and ended up getting better at it. So, your next exercise is to look at your own goals and establish for all of them, especially your major goals, what your quitability point is going to be. One goal is not to give up on the Ten Steps.'

I looked at my watch and noticed how the time had flown by. It was now 10 pm.

'Let's have an early night,' I said thinking of Isabella, 'but before we go let's just spend ten minutes doing our exercises. All you have to do is write your goal and then write what your quitability point is. You won't complete it all, I just want to get you started, and then you can go home and finish them off. However, you have to promise me you will finish them tonight, while you are in the right frame of mind.

'Yes we will, Michael, you are beginning to sound like my mum and dad,' joked Brianna.

'Thank you for the compliment, Brianna' and with that, we all spent ten minutes on our exercise.

When the ten minutes were up, Ade, Lian, Matt and Brianna got up to leave.

Ade put his hand on my shoulder, looked me in the eye and said 'Thank you, Michael for sharing these Ten Steps with us. I feel like I can achieve anything that I put my mind to now. I wouldn't have missed this opportunity for anything.'

'I have done nothing. I am just reaching out to help others, anyone can do that. Thanks anyway and see you all tomorrow.'

Whilst everyone was saying their goodbyes, Lian said that they would host our group the following evening.

Go to the exercises for Chapter 8

CHAPTER NINE

Time out

After everyone left, Isabella and I tided up. *'You were so animated tonight Michael, it's been a long time since I've seen you like that. That's what attracted me to you.'*

'I know what you are saying Isabella, I've just got lost in all the problems and pressures we have had. I lost focus and I lost my personality. However, with the help of the Ten Steps, you will never see that side of me again.' Isabella went up to the bed. 'I'll be up in a moment.'

I couldn't help but think how great things were between Isabella and me. We were getting on together, better than we had been for a long time. We had been through a lot together, but we seemed to have grown apart. Will we be able to rebuild our love and companionship? Would the present last? I knew our love was worth fighting for. We both had to change, especially me.

Just then, Isabella walked into the living room in a sexy negligee, and it was the one I had brought for her birthday two years ago.

'Is everything okay?' I said.

'Yes,' said Isabella, with a twinkle In her eyes. I put my arms around her and looked into her eyes. *'I was thinking that so much has happened these last few days. Ten days ago we were talking about splitting up, and now I feel like a teenager in love again.'*

'Isabella you are so beautiful' we kissed. 'I just want to apologise for the heartache I've caused you. I hope you can forgive me?'

'I hope that you can forgive me too,' said Isabella, *'I know that I have not been the most understanding at times…'*

'Shush,' I said, and then we kissed passionately.

Getting up is a slow process. I got myself ready for work. Isabella got Emilio and Jason prepared for school. We kissed and hugged, and off I went to work.

Today was a quiet day for me at work. It dawned on me that I was so busy sorting everyone else's life out that I had forgotten about my own goals and aspirations. I hadn't had time to reflect on the Ten Steps. Since that first night, it has been like a whirlwind between work, our meetings every night and family. I decided that I needed time out. I looked up at the clock on the office wall. It was 4 pm. I decided to cancel tonight's meeting at Ade's house.

I walked through the office to Ade's desk and discreetly explained how I felt, and I thought it was better if we all had a night to ourselves to reflect on our goals and exercises to bring them up to date.

Ade agreed and explained how he had neglected a few chores and that this would also give him time. He also said that Lian's Mum was visiting them tomorrow, so she would be able to babysit, but they wouldn't be able to hold the meeting there.

'Just make sure that you do not neglect those steps, because that's what we end up doing in life; putting our future on hold for the present or past.'

'I won't,' said Ade.

I sent a group message to the others explaining that tonight would be cancelled for everyone to work on the exercises, and we would meet up at mine and Isabella's place the following evening.

I quickly received replies from Matt and Brianna, both saying that they were disappointed but that they were looking forward to meeting up again the following night.

I got home at my usual time, and Isabella was writing. I was glad to be home; I hugged Isabella and quickly explained that I had cancelled tonight and told everyone that we would be having the meeting at our house the following evening. *'That's fine for everyone to come here, but I can't believe that you cancelled the meeting. Why did you do that?'* Isabella said in a surprised manner.

'Well, so much has happened; I just felt that we needed some time to reflect on the work that we have done so far. To tell the truth, I needed time to reflect on the Ten Steps myself. So much had changed in the last week, I mean both of us last week were on the verge of a separation and now we are madly in love again.' I paused and looked Isabella in the eyes. I lowered my voice and said softly, 'I hope that you are still in love with me Isabella?'

'Yes I am – of course I am,' said Isabella, and she kissed me. *'I've always been in love with you. It's just been the stress and pressure we've been under, not to mention our lack of communication recently.'*

'I know we always seem to be arguing...' I said, '... and that is one of the things I would like us to do tonight is to express our feelings and try to find some common goals together. We can work on the Ten Steps together.'

'Right, you sort Emilio and Jason out, I'll finish dinner and then we can sit down and do the Ten Steps together,' Isabella said.

As I played with the boys and then dressed them for bed, I couldn't help but think how complicated our lives are as adults and how simple a child's life was. Their priorities in life were having as much fun as they could. But what is life without some fun! Every day was a new adventure.

What happened? I had swapped my adventures as a kid for nightmares as an adult.

Just then, Isabella called, *'Dinner is ready.'*

We all sat down together at the table and enjoyed a lovely meal. The boys could sense that something was different as they were very animated and chatting about their day at school, and we all joined in laughter when Jason told us about something funny that he had seen during his day. After dinner, I washed up whilst Isabella took the boys up to bed and settled them down for the night.

Isabella asked, *'Where shall we begin?'* when we were comfortably sitting in the living room.

'I think we should start with us and go through the Ten Steps together. I know we are not going to agree on everything, so let's start with what we want out of our relationship.'

Isabella looked at me for a second and then said, *'I want companionship, someone to share my life with. I want to be happy and I want Emilio and Jason to be happy and grow up to be well-balanced people. I want to travel; I'd like some new clothes, a bigger house so that the boys can have their own separate bedrooms. I don't know, Michael; I just want the simple things in life.'*

'Simple things!' I remarked. 'Well, that's what the goal-setting exercise is for. I want the same things, but maybe I'm more materialistic and want a luxurious lifestyle. However, I know that all goals have a cost, and they cost time, money, and effort.

'Our problem recently has been that we have been struggling to get out of debt, pay bills, cut back, deprive ourselves of some of the luxuries to survive. We have dug ourselves a hole, and our efforts have been digging us deeper with the hole to the point where we can't see reason. The Ten Steps offer us a way out, a way to change our situation, but that will take time, love, faith and understanding, or we have nothing.

'I love you, Isabella, but sometimes you make a big fuss about the little things. I'm not criticising you because I know I wind you up too. We are both guilty. I hate that word guilty. Should I say, we are both at fault. That's just as bad. For example, we may fall out or argue over leaving the lights on in the kitchen or whatever. I'm not leaving the lights on, on purpose, I'm not…

'That's not fair Michael; I'm just concerned about wasting electricity and keeping the bills down because we can't afford it.'

'I know but our love is worth more than a few pence on the electricity.'

'I know Michael, but it all adds up.'

'Yes it does, but we both have habits that annoy one another and I know when we are stressed it's harder to accept or tolerate each other's little idiosyncrasies. Then that drives tension between us and one thing leads to the other, and before you know it, we are not talking TO each other we are talking AT each other, and our communication channels are down, all because I left the light on which is silly.

'I also know that you have had to make some sacrifices based on my career and my own ambitions, but that's why we need to start again and use the Ten Steps together. The more we are in harmony together with what we want and where we want to go with our lives, the more we will understand each other's goals. What is important to us and the answer is to support each other. What I mean is that if I know something is really important to you then it's easier for me to support you and accept it and vice versa. Do you understand Isabella?'

Isabella paused for a few seconds. She looked sad, her head was down, and her eyes became glossy. Then she dropped the bomb. She lifted her head and looked at me, and in a sad, soft voice, she said, *'What if we have totally different goals and we want different things? What then, what do we do? Michael, I'm scared of the possibility that we might not be compatible anymore. As relationships develop, we can grow or evolve in and out of harmony ending up at the same emotional point together or in totally different places.'*

'Don't be daft,' I said, but in the back of my mind, I knew the same thought had entered my head in the past, and I had resisted it.

'Well, this is how I see it, Isabella. This is our opportunity to test our love. This is our opportunity to find out if we will be happy, or pretend we have an okay relationship because we are scared to face reality and then five, ten plus years down the road get divorced. Well, that's the same now. Let's focus on our love and work everything out.

'We have a lovely house, two beautiful sons, and a good standard of living. We have just been living a little above our means. We have some excellent friends, we have each other and what a future we are going to have!'

'We've had some great holidays as well haven't we? Do you remember when we went to Greece for the first time?'

'Yes, I do,' said Isabella. *'Michael the more you mention the good times, the more that I remember. We have had some really good times haven't we?'* said Isabella.

'Yes we have, that's the spirit and now we are wiser and stronger and together we can take anything on.'

We talked until midnight; it was the first time that Isabella and I had discussed so many issues without arguing. Don't get me wrong we agreed to disagree on a few points, but overall, we now know what each other's goals are and how to interpret them.

'The last time we did anything like this, Isabella, was when we were starting out. Remember how it felt? How exciting it was?'

Isabella smiled and nodded.

We got up from the sofa, turned off the light, and made our way up to bed.

Once we were in bed, Isabella cuddled into me. It was a great feeling that we were together as one.

CHAPTER TEN

Step Eight: Accept full responsibility for the outcome of your goals

The following morning saw the usual routine. I would put the coffee pot on, Isabella would make breakfast for us all, I would clear away the dishes and then we would both dress the boys. I couldn't help but think how every morning was a little tense, but amidst all the chaos and pressures, by 9 am Emilio and Jason were at school and I'm at work. Isn't it amazing when you have a predetermined goal with a date and time, no matter what, you achieve it more or less on time? I must remember this for our meeting tonight. Just being able to sit down and talk things over with Isabella had revived me. I hope they all feel the same as I do; refreshed.

At 7.30 pm Isabella and I sat down with a glass of red wine to have a few minutes together. I was ready for **Step Eight**.

At 7.45 pm the doorbell rang, it was Matt, *'I'm sorry I'm early, I really missed our meeting yesterday. These Ten Steps have been the making of me. Did you know that I had a pool tournament two nights ago and I didn't go.'*

'You didn't? You should have,' I said.

'I love pool, but sorting my life out is more important, isn't it, Michael?'

'Yes, it is.' Just then the doorbell rang and Ade, Lian and Brianna turned up together. We said our hellos and engaged in a bit of general chitchat. Everyone had a drink and was in good spirits. We settled down. We all sounded refreshed from the little break of the previous night.

'Okay shall we get started? **Step Eight is about accepting full responsibility**

for the outcome of your goal. Whatever happens, you accept full responsibility for the outcome. Remember "If it's to be, it's up to me." The buck stops right here, with you.

'But what if it's not our fault?' said Matt.

'It doesn't matter; you are responsible whatever the result, when you blame or pass the buck, you pass your power over. If you don't accept responsibility at the beginning then you have an excuse. What can you give as an example of something that might have been your fault?'

'What if the bus is late and that makes me late: it is not my fault, I was at the bus stop on time?' Matt said.

'Yes that is true in one sense, but if you had accepted full responsibility for getting there on time, you would have started out earlier and planned to catch the earlier bus wouldn't you?'

'Yes,' said Matt, *'I see.'*

'What accepting responsibility is about – is that people let you down so don't take chances; catch the earlier bus to be on the safe side. Let me ask you this question, have you been in a pool tournament and played a bad shot?'

'Yes, I have.'

'Whose fault was it for the bad shot? The table, the balls, your opponent? No one's was it? You accept full responsibility for the bad shot, you miscalculated and all you can do is learn from it, keep your calm and try and make up for it on your next turn.'

'Yes, I see what you mean because I have done that before, blamed the table, the pots too tight, you know, then got angry with myself and my game just went downhill from there.'

'Well that's what happens when we blame or pass the buck, we go downhill.

'Now, accepting the responsibility for your actions is not blaming yourself. We've covered this already. It's not saying I should have known better and filling yourself with guilt or criticising yourself.'

You see, you can question your performance, but not your ability. When you criticise, blame or feel guilty, you are destroying your confidence and belief in yourself. Knowing what we know now, we'll never do that again will we?'

'*No.*' everyone said in unison.

'But! You still have to be aware because even if you don't criticise yourself, someone else might. For example your wife, partner, friends, boss, the public or that voice in your head. We are mostly taught in society by our parents, teachers, family, friends, TV etc. These are our main areas of influence, that therefore when we make a mistake, instead of learning from it, we are made to feel guilty and sometimes ridiculed.

'Think back to when we were all children. Did you ever do something wrong at school and got ridiculed in front of the class? So, guess what, we learn to pass the blame or guilt. We are afraid to accept responsibility for the simplest things. I'll give you a good example of that.

'Organising a day out with a dear friend. There's always the thought that if it's a flop, I'll get the blame, so it's better to opt out and let someone else do it. So, if it goes wrong you can blame them. I know I've done that myself several times. Well every time you do that, you give your power away and weaken your confidence and that's why we don't set goals. If we don't achieve these goals then we feel guilty, it reminds us of the hundreds of things we said we were going to do and didn't do. They say a hero dies only once, but a coward dies a thousand deaths. We must learn to accept full responsibility and then do our best to make sure the worst doesn't happen.

'Responsibility when you look at the word it means the ability to respond…

'**There is a direct relationship between accepting responsibility for us in a positive role and feeling good about yourself.** People who seem to be in control of their lives are happier people. We tend to make excuses for our lives instead of taking control. **We are totally 100% responsible for our own lives.** Accepting responsibility helps us to find answers quicker, and helps us resolve our problems quickly. The only way we can stop blaming, criticising or feeling guilty personally is to learn to love ourselves. Love is our greatest gift. You must listen to the song, 'The Greatest Love of All' by George Benson; it's a great song. Loving and accepting ourselves of our fears, uncertainties, doubts, resentments etc.

'I read somewhere that there are over fifty negative superstitions that we carry.'

Matt jumped in, *'I bet I've had all of these.'*

Everyone laughed.

'So one of the exercises we need to do is learn to start loving yourself by saying to yourself, **'I love and approve of myself'** hundreds of times, every day. Try it now and notice how you feel.'

I paused for a second. 'It feels uncomfortable doesn't it? What is wrong with liking yourself?' I asked.

Ade answered, *'it will make you big-headed.'*

'You see that is the problem. When we see someone who is in control they know what they want and go after it, we call them egotistical, but underneath we probably envy them. Don't get me wrong, some are but I'm not asking you to be big-headed, I'm asking you to look into the mirror of your mind and see a loving person who is accepting responsibility for themselves, whatever you are faced with. Any negative emotion or situation, say to yourself, "I am responsible, I am responsible, I am responsible." We need to learn to use positive affirmations to enhance our confidence and build our self-esteem.'

'Talking of which, it's time to do another exercise. Now this is a quick exercise; make a list of ten of your goals that you take full responsibility for.

For example, I accept full responsibility for achieving my goal of losing ten pounds in weight in the next three months. Do you all understand?'

'Yes we do,' everyone said.

'Right you have ten minutes and I'll make everyone a drink.'

Go to exercises at the end of Chapter 10

'Are you all finished?' I said as I gave everyone their drinks,

'Yes we are.'

'The next exercise is to make a list of all the things, people etc you are angry at, things that you hate, are jealous about etc. Okay let's take five minutes and make a list.' I could see in their faces that they were not expecting any exercises.

I got up and quickly left the room before everyone could say anything. Who was I angry with? I asked myself. I was angry with my dad, my uncle, my school, my boss at work, myself. I had been angry with Isabella, but I realised now, it was my responsibility and I forgave everyone.

Five minutes went by and I returned to our living room. Everyone's face had changed, they looked angry. 'Take a quick look at your faces, can you see the anger? You see, every time we get angry or harbour a negative emotion, we take it out on ourselves. We have to stop that and the only way that we can do that is to learn to forgive.'

'I can never forgive my dad for what he did to me,' said Ade.

'What did he do?'

'He walked out on my mum, when I was nine years old, I will never forgive him for that.'

'How does that anger make you feel?'

'Well, I feel annoyed, betrayed, let down.'

'I'm sorry for this, Ade but I need to use this situation as an example is that okay with you?'

'Yes,' he replied.

'How old are you now.'

'I am thirty-eight years old.'

'So you have been carrying all that' pain for nineteen years. Do you like hurting yourself?'

'NO!'

'How often do you think about it now?'

'Not so much now, but I used to think about it all the time as a child…'

'Let me ask you a question, if I gave you a needle would you prick yourself all over your body several times a day?'

'Don't be silly, why would I do that to myself?'

'Well that is what you are doing every time you think of your dad. Can't you see that you are the only one suffering and it's holding you back? I know it's difficult and now is not the time, but you have to make the time and forgive him, you have to say the words, "Dad I forgive you." Now you don't have to say that to his face so long as you do it and mean it. Learning to forgive will free you. You have mourned long enough; it's time to move on.

'You see that's another problem we are taught to hold onto negative emotions. I said this earlier, There is a saying in the Bible I've always loved, 'He who is without sin, cast the first stone' we have all hurt another human being somewhere, conscious or unconscious that's why you must forgive or the pain of not letting go won't let you be happy.

143

'Forgiving doesn't mean you have to like them, but you will like yourself more. On your way home tonight, say these words to yourself, "I like myself and 'I forgive… for they know not what they do." It's about letting go and making more room in your heart for love.

You know the Disney kids movie? Let it go, let it go, let it go.

'Have you ever had a little child destroy something that was important to you? As angry as you were, you forgave them, why? They didn't know what they were doing. Most adults are just babies with old faces. If you can forgive a baby, you can forgive an adult. The crime is to keep returning to the person or situation that hurts you and reliving it. Forgive and move on. Let it go…

'To forgive we need to love ourselves more. The power of love will never be underestimated.

'There's a story I heard from Brian Tracy, a great educational and motivational speaker about an experiment that took place in the early part of the 1900s. They took children that were born in deprived areas and split them into groups. Group one was continually held, given affection, a caring environment etc. and the second group had their nappies changed and they were fed, but they were never talked to or held and were deliberately not shown any emotion as babies. Are you ready for this? Well in one of the experiments, which had to be stopped and it was stopped too late, most of the children in the second group died. They died of a lack of love.

'That's unbelievable,' said Lian.

'I know. The need for love is so crucial to our development in our first few years. You see without love, somehow we wouldn't have made it, so we must learn to love ourselves, "I love and approve of myself" are two affirmations you can use, make some up for yourself.'

'God gave me all I need to succeed,' said Lian.

'I am happy,' said Matt.

'The list goes on… You see if we don't as adults learn to love ourselves, we shall shrivel up. One of the greatest crimes in the world today, that has killed more people than all the wars put together is the feeling of being unloved, helplessness, feeling alone. All the negative emotions that we all carry around.'

'This is heavy stuff,' said Matt.

'I know but can you see the importance. **To accept responsibilities is to empower yourself and to do that you must love and approve of yourself, believe in yourself and learn to forgive yourself and others.**

'Nobody is perfect. Nobody so when you mess up, pick yourself up, learn the lesson so you are wiser and forgive yourself.

'You all know my Christian beliefs and I'm not preaching to you, but God sent his son Jesus to help us and sacrificed him so that we might be forgiving for our own sins. Is that not one of the greatest stories about love for us? Even Jesus on the cross before he died said those famous words, "Father forgive them for they know not what they do"'

'Forgive and you release all the anger, pain and hurt you have been carrying around for years… it is not easy I know but you are forgiving for your sake, not theirs. You are releasing yourself to be happier and more fulfilled.

'You can write a letter forgiving them, you can post it or just writing it helps, you can write it down on a paper and then burn the paper as a sign of the end or tell them face to face. Just simply let it go, forgive and free yourself… Do it for yourself, because you deserve to be free and happier.

'Does this make sense?'

'Yes,' replied everyone.

Brianna said, *'I've never looked at forgiveness that way …it's not easy but I will try.'*

'Right, that's it for tonight don't forget to do your exercises:

1. Write down a list of positive affirmations. You need to repeat several times a day. Learn to love and approve of yourself.
2. Make a list of all the things, people, circumstances etc that you are angry, envious, jealous etc. with these.
3. Forgive or learn to forgive all the people and circumstances that you make a list of.
4. Accept full responsibility for yourself from now on and whenever any negative things happen, say to yourself, **'I am responsible' I am responsible' I am responsible.'** Look for a solution, look at your goals and accept responsibility to make sure that you achieve them.'

We all said our goodnights and everyone left. I turned to Isabella, 'Wow, that was draining tonight. I hope that they got it.'

'Well judging by how quiet they were, I think they took it in. I get it; I have to accept responsibility for a situation. I have always coped and achieved and when I don't I get stressed.'

'Thanks, Isabella. I'm so pleased and relieved that you understand. Let's quickly tidy the cups and glasses away and get to bed. I have a feeling it won't take us long to drop off to sleep tonight.'

Before I knew it, morning had broken. It was another sunny spring day. As I lay there for a few moments, I thought to myself that I am glad to be alive. I am one of the lucky ones – I woke up today. Some people in the world wouldn't have made it through the night...

Always start your day by counting your blessings.

We are all blessed in many ways.

CHAPTER ELEVEN

Step Nine: Taking action on our goals and having the discipline to follow through

It was my turn to drop Emilio and Jason off at school. As the boys walked away from the car and through the school gates, I couldn't help but think how we get conditioned by the system. The system, in a lot of cases, does not prepare us for the real world. We are brought up to conform to this model, yet every one of us is born different, each one of us an individual with a completely different and unique DNA.

We have all our goals that are exciting to us but then get bogged down with responsibilities and debts, then we start living under the circumstances instead of above them. It's amazing how many there are out there if you look for them. I am seeing the world differently now; it's like having x-ray vision. My mind kept wandering, but as I got closer to work, I began to focus on my day. I had a couple of meetings today and an appraisal with my boss. I was going to ask about promotion prospects, a pay rise and about what I need to do to get it.

I arrived at work and settled down to my usual routine. My life or should I say my lifestyle had become a habit and if I was going to succeed, I would need to change some of my habits. There's that frightening word, again – **Change**. I was ready; I have a new focus and direction in life now.

My day went well, especially with my appraisal and promotion request. I couldn't wait to tell Isabella the good news. I got home full of excitement and positivity but the moment that I opened the front door I was met with, what can only be described as a major battlefield; Emilio and Jason were playing up. *'The boys are refusing to do their homework, all they want to do is to play with their toys!'* Isabella was losing her cool and now I was starting to as well.

Isn't it great being a parent, I thought sarcastically. Well, I suppose it goes with the territory as I smiled to myself. How could little humans cause so much stress in minutes? Just then Isabella shrieked, *'I've burnt the dinner! You see what both of you have done now?'*

I tried to calm down the situation. I sat the boys on the sofa and gave them a stern look. I asked them both if they liked being unhappy. They both said that they didn't. Then I asked if they liked Mummy being unhappy, and they looked at their feet and said 'No, Daddy, we don't.' I told them that their actions today had upset Mummy, and now we need to make her happy again. I helped them to tidy away their toys into the toy box, and sat them both at the table with their schoolwork. When they had settled into doing their homework, I went into the kitchen. Isabella had her back to me. I wrapped my arms around her waist and spun her around, then planted a kiss on her lips. She smiled. We both knew that silence was the best policy at that moment, otherwise an argument about the boys may ensue again.

We had a lovely dinner, albeit being a little burned. I said I liked my food caramelised occasionally… which brought a laugh to the table.

After we had eaten Isabella took the boys to bed and I left for the meeting. Isabella was unable to go as we couldn't get a babysitter.

In all the confusion I forgot to mention the pay rise and promotion prospects.

It was time for me to focus on our meeting tonight. We have done a lot of talking and writing. It was now time to act. I arrived at Ade's place. I was the last to get there. I greeted everyone and Lian made me a cup of tea and we settled down.

Matt was the first to speak, *'I can't believe we are near the end, I'm really going to miss our meetings.'*

'Well Matt, remember what we have learnt. There are no ends just beginnings. As one thing ends another begins, this must be our new way of thinking. It's just another chapter in your life. There is no end and most religions believe that we continue in another world or reincarnate or whatever the explanation, there is no end, only a new rainbow for us to follow.

Isn't that an exciting way of living our lives?'

'It's an exciting way but also frightening because you never know what's around the corner.'

'Yes, I agree, but that is the cautious, pessimistic side of us. That's why if we follow our goals and dreams we can control more of what is around the corner. Imagine driving a car, with no steering wheel, how would you get from A to B?'

'It will be by accident,' said Matt.

'It's easy to manoeuvre a car once you are in control of the car, and so it is easier to control what's around the corner when you are in control of your life.'

'Let me give you another example. Have you noticed when you want to buy a particular car, how all of a sudden you see that make and model of car everywhere you go? You see the adverts, brochures, anything to do with that car and brand…'

'You're absolutely right,' said Ade.

'… and you notice every detail, colour, make, etc. Have you noticed that when you eventually buy the car and your focus has moved on? You notice the car, but not the same way that you did before. Once we have focused on a goal, we start noticing everything in relation to that goal. Now if that goal is negative, we notice all the negative things that happen around us. Imagine you didn't know which car you wanted, it would be difficult to focus, and it would take longer to make your mind up.

'We need however to get back to what we are focusing on today and that's **Step Nine**.'

'The Step Nine is about **'Taking action on our goals and having the discipline to follow through.'** As the old Chinese proverb goes, 'A journey of a 1000 steps begins with the first step.' The first step has been the easy part. That is doing the exercises and research, finding out what you want to do with your life, your goals, your aspirations, but now we have to put it into action. Procrastination is one of the biggest crimes we humans make. How many times have you had an idea about something and did nothing about it, only to find years down the road, somebody else has had the same idea, taken action and got it manufactured and distributed?'

'That's so true,' said Matt. *'As an electrician, I've had several ideas, but never did anything about it, only to find it being done by someone else in the future.'*

'This is a very important point in our life. **A goal or dream without 'action' is a wish.** The seeds of greatness will avoid you if you are not **disciplined to take action.** We must put all our plans into action. Nothing happens until we take action. Action, this reminds me of a story I heard once. There was this horse, a hardworking horse that had been put out to graze in the field. A bee used to enjoy flying around the horse's head and annoying him. One day the horse got fed up, he was sick and tired of the bee annoying him so he hatched a plan. "What I need to do is catch the bee with my mouth and swallow him that will teach the bee a lesson." So, the horse began practising a quick turn of his head and a quick bite. Eventually, he was ready. The big day came and the bumblebee started to annoy the horse; the horse was ready, he had a plan of action. The bee came along and buzzed around his head, annoying the horse and then all of a sudden the horse turned his head quickly and swallowed the bee.

'It was lights out for the bee. The horse was proud of himself. The plan had worked. The bee, however, was confused, what happened he was in total darkness and the smell was unbelievable. Eventually, it dawned on the bee what had happened, he was in the horse's stomach. "I can't believe it, that foolish horse swallowed me." At this point the bee began to get very angry; I'm going to show that horse that he had messed with the wrong bee. "I'm going to sting him with my biggest sting ever. In fact this is going to be a big job, the biggest of my life. I'm going to need all my strength. I know what I am going to do. I'll have a little rest, charge up my batteries and get all my strength together for tomorrow."

'So, he went to sleep. He woke up the next day, only to find himself covered in this sticky smelly green/brown mess on the grass and the horse was gone. Yes, you guessed it, the horse was gone and the bee ended up in the horse's excrement. The moral of the story is if you don't take action when you are supposed to you could end up in a pile of poop. So do today what you can, because you don't know what tomorrow will bring.'

'I get it,' said Matt. *'If you don't take action now, you can end up in someone else's excrement.'*

'That is another way of putting it. Everything we love or see around us is because someone, or we, took action. We took action to be here today. The bee knew what he had to do, he just didn't have the discipline to follow through.'

'In a lot of cases we know what we are supposed to do but we are afraid of doing it, just in case it might be wrong. Someone once said to me that we are only born with two fears, the fear of falling and the fear of loud noises. We have no other fears at birth. All the fears we face today are taught. One of the reasons why we don't take **action** is because we are afraid of the outcome. We have been conditioned with certain boundaries. Some of these boundaries were set when we were children to protect us, but it's up to us with the help of the steps to free ourselves.

'This reminds me of the story of the elephant and the Banyan tree. In India, what they do when the elephant is a baby is they tie a chain around one of its legs and tie the other end to a tree. The tree is massive with very deep roots. The baby elephant pulls and tugs and tries to escape, the chains are cutting into his legs. Eventually he is in so much pain, he gives up and accepts that for as long as the chain is wrapped around his leg he will never escape.

'Years on you see this large elephant being ridden by a tourist. He or she could take a building down, crush a car and all they have to secure the elephant is a rope tied around its leg, which is pegged into the grass. The elephant doesn't realise he/she can escape because every time they tug on the rope, they remember what it was like with the chains and although he/she is bigger and stronger now, they only remember the place and the conditions.

So it is with us, that although we are bigger and stronger, we only remember the pain of the past. We are conditioned, so that we don't take action today; we give up before we even try. There are so many examples.'

'This reminds me of a game of pool I had in a tournament,' said Matt. *'There was a shot I needed to play to win the game, but I had missed a similar shot before. So I took the safe shot and lost. To this day I still regret taking the safe shot.'*

'One of the definitions of action in the dictionary is expedience of energy. Nothing happens unless we take action. It is difficult to take action when you don't know what you want to achieve isn't it? We must have the discipline to stick to our goals and beliefs. In the dictionary again the definition for discipline is training that produces orderliness, obedience and self-control. Remember we are all born successful but we need to be disciplined to take action on our goals to fulfil our dreams.

'We are now a nation of procrastinators, we use words such as if, when, but, tomorrow, let me think about it, I'll do it next week, etc. to hold us back.

'All successful people are doers; they say if you want something done, give it to a busy person because they will get it done. Give it to someone who procrastinates and they will give you an excuse, why it can't be done.'

'We have to get into the "Do it now" programme. Isabella is very good at that, she's always trying to get me to do job's around the house now,' I said with a smile on my face.

'I know the feeling,' Ade said jokingly.

'Let's summarise what we have to do. **Step Nine is about taking action on our goals and having the discipline to follow through** regardless. The time for action is now, we must take action now.

'I would like us to do a little exercise. We need to make a list of ten top things we can take action on now.'

'Now?' said Matt,

'Yes, now! There is no time like now. Let's not procrastinate. Look at your goals, plans, aspirations and make a list of ten items to take action on your action list.

'One action could be to make a phone call when you leave here to someone in your family you haven't spoken to for years, to a lost friend. It could be an apology. It's time for us all to take action on things that we have been putting off.

'I'll give you an example, after my first night of the Ten Steps, I wrote a long letter to my dad. I found it easier to explain myself better. We hadn't talked for four years, I don't want to go into the why, but after I finished the letter I cried, it was like a big weight off my shoulders. There are bridges we have burnt that need repairing.'

'A similar thing happened with my brother, we fell out over my car. He borrowed and crashed my car. Then he didn't want to pay for it,' said Ade. *'We didn't speak for years, till one Christmas, when we made up. Do you know we have been better friends since then.'*

'I had a similar situation with my best friend,' said Brianna, *'but when I tried to talk to her she didn't want to know.'*

'Do it for you, not for them, and if they don't want to forgive and forget, at least you can move on knowing you tried. Anyway, that's just one aspect of your action list. So, let's spend fifteen minutes, making a list as long as you can of all the things that you are going to take action on.'

I got up and said, 'Focus on your action list, these are things you are actually going to do and some of them need to be items you can do in the next twenty-four, forty-eight or seventy-two hours. This is your chance to start the new you; this is you in spring time looking forward to a fantastic summer.' And with that, I left the room and went to sit in the kitchen so that they would work alone and not ask questions. These were things that they needed to think about for themselves with no hints or prompts.

Go to the exercises at the end of Chapter 11

153

As I sat there I pulled up my notes app on my phone and looked at the action list I had done over a week ago. There were things I had done over a week ago, but there were also some items I had still not done. I needed to revisit and update them. So, as I waited for the others to start their lists, I went through mine.

Fifteen minutes went by, I walked back into the room; 'By the way, you need to add to your action list the following: one, to read your goals every day and two, to have a weekly action list and a weekly review of where you are at. Discipline is doing what we need to do even though we don't feel like it. This is where the discipline comes in. If you can do this exercise regularly, follow the steps; continue to always reappraise your goals. Who you are, who you want to be, what you want etc; you will have a more fulfilled life.

'I love gardening because you can see the results of your efforts. To have a beautiful garden takes time, planning, action and then patience to let it all come together.'

'Tomorrow is our last day; we need to start putting what we've learnt into action. You were born to win and we were born successful. We must take action **now, today, tonight** and start striving forward. Remember the Chinese proverb; a journey of a thousand steps starts with the first one. Let's take some steps tonight. I think that is a good point to finish tonight. The talking is coming to an end, it's nearly over, we need to move forward.

'Knowledge is only powerful when you use it. If knowledge on its own was powerful, then it would rule the world. Knowledge must lead to action otherwise it is a waste of time. The Ten Steps are not designed just to make you a wise person who does nothing, but a wiser person – one that takes educated and calculated steps forward on purpose.

'Is your life worth fighting for, worth taking chances for and is it worth investing an hour or two or more a week, is it all worth it? Don't answer me,' I said quickly, 'answer yourself. A week from now you could be looking in the mirror and you've gone back to your old ways and used the best of excuses that failures use around the world: I haven't got the time to do it – doesn't work – I tried trying. Trying is an excuse for failure. In an adventure, you don't hear a general in the army saying we are going to try, do you?

'Don't cheat that person in the mirror, your family, and your children. Remember that failure is not an option. Have we got reasons to succeed or excuses to fail? The decision is yours. The time for action is now.

'Time cannot be saved up and used at another date. Let me ask you all a question, if I gave you £86,400 every day to spend, knowing that what was left at the end of each day, would be taken away from you forever. Would you not try your best to spend all of it?'

'I know that I would have no problems,' said Matt.

'Well, let me explain there are twenty-four hours in a day, sixty minutes to an hour and sixty seconds to a minute. When you add all that up together you end up, with 86,400 seconds, to use every day and what you don't use gets taken away from you.'

'That's amazing.' said Ade. *'I've never thought of it that way. In fact it can be quite negative looking at it that way because we have wasted billions.'*

'Again let's focus on the present and the future, not the past. Let's start spending that 86,400 seconds a day on our goals, our life and our families. That's what the Ten Steps are all about, we're making it happen for ourselves.

'Tomorrow is our last day, we will summarise the previous nine steps and I will give you the tenth step, which is simple but can be difficult to do. Isabella and I would like to have you all to our place for the last night.'

'That sounds so final,' said Matt.

'We have come a long way. We will do dinner and would like every one of you at the end to say a few words on what the Ten Steps have meant to you and share an action point you have taken, and lastly why you will commit to the Ten Steps.

'Once again thank you for your time and I hope that you have enjoyed the nine steps so far.'

'Michael you have given me a new perspective on life,' said Matt, *'… and I thank you for that.'*

We all said our goodnights and off we went. Isabella was still up when I got home. *'I'm just making a hot chocolate, do you want one?'*

'No thank you, I think I will have a glass of wine.'

'What's up Michael, you look a little perturbed?'

'I know it has just dawned on me that we are coming to the end and Ade, Lian, Brianna and Matt have been my first students and I don't know if I have done a good job of communicating the Ten Steps and explaining everything to them.'

'Don't doubt yourself Michael. You can't be responsible for their actions and decisions. One of the first things I remember you told me about the Ten Steps is when the voice said to you, "Many call for my help but few listen." The Ten Steps are the Ten Steps. It's like a Treasure Island map, if you don't follow all the directions, you won't find the treasure.'

'You have given them the map; they and only they can make that journey to their Treasure Island.'

'I know, I just want them to realise their true potential.'

'Well the best way to help them, Michael, is by realising our potential.'

'You are right, let's get cracking on with our own goals and action plans.' Isabella and I talked until 2 am. I really enjoyed it when we shared our goals and aspirations together. This was a new beginning, the beginning of an endless journey and I was ready, we were ready.

'You know Isabella; the best part of the Ten Steps so far is that we have got each other back. Oh, and another thing – I didn't mention this earlier as it was a little hectic when I arrived home and it then slipped my mind, but I had my appraisal at work today and things went really really well. I spoke up about a pay rise and promotion. My boss was a little startled at first as I don't think he was expecting the 'new and improved confident me' to take the lead in negotiations.' I let out a little chuckle.

'Really? wow, that IS great news. Let's talk about it in the morning when we're not so tired, but I know what you're saying about sharing our goals and aspirations, I feel the same way, Michael.'

'Our relationships in life are at the top of what we do and how happy we are and that's so important. Let's go to bed,' I said, 'it's a big day tomorrow.' We turned off the lights and headed upstairs to bed.

CHAPTER TWELVE

Step Ten: Share your blessings

The alarm clock rang loudly, and both Isabella and I got up. The sun shone through the window, and I felt so blessed to be alive. Whilst we were in the kitchen, we followed our usual routine. Breakfast with the boys, I had my coffee and orange juice. I set off for work, and Isabella dressed the boys, ready to walk them to school.

As I was driving to work, it dawned on me again that we live our lives within the routines we have created, and after a while, that routine becomes our life. We live in a box that we create until something rocks your world or you decide: I want more.

How do you change that morning routine with the kids, school, bills to pay etc... you can't change it in an instant, but you can start your day earlier to make sure you get time to read your goals, look at your vision board and visualise yourself already achieving them. Start the day with the kids at breakfast and talk about what we are grateful for today. Start your day with a reminder of all you are thankful for. Start a gratitude list. In our lives, we can upgrade and improve our routines, which will upgrade us.

Just as I reflected on this, I didn't realise I had actually arrived at work.

Work, yes, work, another routine. I had some projects to complete, a Zoom meeting with a new client. It was going to be a busy but productive day. I felt different. I was working with a purpose rather than just doing a job... no wonder I probably didn't get promoted in the past – I was a pessimist and only did as much as was needed.

In a quiet voice, I said to myself repeatedly, 'Reflect on where I am today, this moment. Thank you, thank you, thank you for waking up the sleeping giant in me.'

I remembered that night with the voice – many call for help, but few listen... I am so glad I listened and took onboard the lessons of life from my higher power from the universe. Life is good. I mean, life is really good when you look at your blessings.

We are truly blessed so we can bless others. But until you feel blessed, it's hard to bless others...

'Michael, Michael!' my boss said. I had drifted off. 'Where is the report you promised?'

'Sorry, I was just thinking about something.' I didn't want him to know where my mind was.

'Back to work, Michael,' he said.

The day went fast. I noticed how Ade and Brianna were buzzing at their work, and they wanted to know what the last step was.

'The last step is... I'll tell you tonight,' I said with a smile.

The day passed by in a flash. I got all I wanted to do at work done and was ready to do the last step. I felt sad but relieved as I drove home, sad that the meeting up with the team – yes, we had become a team – was coming to an end and relieved because it had been intense. I needed time for me, Isabella and the family.

I was so happy to get home and see my family. I walked through the door, gave Isabella a big kiss and cuddled the boys.

'How is everyone today?' I said in a cheerful voice.

'Ermm… you need to speak with your son,' said Isabella. 'He was rude to his teacher today at school.'

'I see, Isabella, when they are naughty they are my sons…' I said with a smile '…and when they are good they are yours…'

I turned to the boys. 'Which one of you is it?'

Jason shouted, 'It's Emilio. Emilio has been naughty.'

'Now Jason, we have said this before: you don't point the finger at anyone, because you too, are not an angel all the time, are you? You do naughty things too, don't you?'

Jason put his head down and said, 'Sorry.'

'Well don't say sorry to me, apologise to Emilio.'

'Sorry Emilio,' Jason said.

'Ok Emilio, what did you do?' I said with a stern face.

'I called the teacher a liar.'

'You did what? Why did you call her a liar?'

'She said we would play a game and later changed her mind and made us do some work instead, I was really looking forward to the game!'

'Well sometimes in life our plans change and you need to deal with the change but you don't get angry and burst out. I'm sure your teacher had a good reason for changing her mind. Just because you don't understand what is happening doesn't mean it's bad. Now make sure you apologise and think before you react next time. Will you do that please?'

'Yes, daddy,' Emilio said in a sad voice and looked down at his feet.

'Emilio I know you are a good person, you just need to learn to think before you react… With that said let's get ready for dinner and bed, we have some guests coming round tonight for dinner and a meeting so I need you to be on your best behaviour. Please can you do that boys?'

'Yes,' they both replied.

I sorted the boys out with their dinner and dressed them in their pyjamas. Isabella finished cooking the meal that we would share with our guests and went to change. I couldn't help thinking about the conversation with Emilio. That was how I reacted before the Ten Steps came into my life.

I would get angry, blame others, not accept responsibility, only see my side… maybe Emilio was mimicking how he had seen me behave. I needed to be more careful in the future, showing the wrong emotions around the boys.

I settled the kids down and tidied up.

Isabella and I were prepared for our guests to go through the final step, and I wondered how they would all react. Isabella had cooked a tasty vegetarian chilli with rice and a delicious vegetarian lasagne in our electric skillet. We had invested in the Saladmaster special cooking system a few years ago in our quest to eat healthier and give the kids a healthier start in life. The food in Saladmaster tastes so fresh and amazing.

The kids enjoyed the chilli as it wasn't too spicy, but I like to spice it up with my red hot chilli sauce when I eat it.

'Isabella, the food smells delicious, I'm hungry.'

'You will just have to wait until everyone is here,' she replied.

We poured a glass of wine and chatted till the doorbell went.

'Hi Brianna and Matt.' They had turned up together. As they walked in, I couldn't help but think how close they were beginning to get… Matt brought a bottle of wine which we opened and chatted with each other. Shortly after,

Ade and Lian turned up. Lian had baked a cheesecake. Cheesecake is one of my absolute favourite desserts. Tonight was going to be a treat...

Now that everyone was here, I spoke to the team. 'Well, the format for tonight is a working dinner... What I mean is that we will serve the food buffet style. Isabella has made vegetarian chilli and brown basmati rice and a vegetarian lasagne in the skillet. I hope you like vegetarian food. We started cooking and eating more vegetarian dishes over the last few years since we got our Saladmaster system. Not that you can only cook vegetarian meals in it, you can cook anything you want to, but we have chosen to take what we feel to be a healthier path for us and the boys.

'What's Saladmaster?' said Matt? 'I'm not a vegetarian person.'

'Matt, just taste the food, and you will be surprised how tasty it is. If you don't like it, I'll order you a takeaway.

'The format tonight is to help yourself to food, grab a glass of wine, then recap the nine steps and finish on the tenth step. Hopefully, by that time, we will get to eat Lian's cheesecake.'

Everyone put some food on their plates, and they all had a bit of both. Matt took the smallest portion – this was going to be a test on Isabella's cooking. I was last to get mine and sit down.

'First, before we start, I just want to propose a toast to all of us for sticking in there and completing the nine steps. That is an achievement we should all be proud of.'

We all toasted our glasses. 'Cheers!'

Then Ade mentioned that we still had the tenth step to do. He wanted to know what it was.

'No problem, Ade, let's enjoy our friendship. I will let you have it, it's a small thing but massive returns to you.'

'*Ok,*' said Ade. '*I would like to propose a toast to our friendship, I have shared things with you that I haven't even shared with my family. Lian and I feel blessed to be part of this team. Here's to friendship!*' We all toasted our glasses together and exclaimed, 'To friendship!'

'Let's eat, I'm hungry.' We all started eating and generally chatting, and after a minute or two, everyone congratulated Isabella on how tasty the food was.

Isabella smiled and said, 'Thank you, but It's not just me, it's my Saladmaster system. It's so easy to use and the food tastes so good. It's made using surgical grade titanium.'

'Oooh, you will have to explain it more to me another time, as we have Step Ten to go through this evening,' Lian said.

Matt piped up, '*Can I have some more please?*'

'Yes, of course,' said Isabella.

'I told you that you would like Isabella's cooking,' I said.

'*I know, it tastes so nice and healthy!*'

'Make sure you leave some for me,' said Ade.

As we all settled down to dinner and general chitchat I interrupted, and I said that I was sure that they all would agree with me that the last eleven days had been somewhat life-changing, and what I mean from that it has been a paradigm shift on how we look at our lives, our old beliefs and our new beliefs.

'We now see our future differently. We started with Step One – accept who you are and where you are today as a beginning. Step Two – what is your life all about and what is your purpose? Step Three – determine what your goals are and set new goals. Step Four – establish people's help and support you will need to achieve your goals. Step Five – believe in yourself and your goals, why not you?. Step Six – take your key goals and make a plan. Step Seven – establish your quitability point. Step Eight – accept full responsibility for the outcome of your goals. Step Nine is taking action on your new goals and have the discipline to follow through.'

Lian said, *'Wow, we have come a long way in eleven days.'*

'I know,' said Brianna. *'We have covered a lot, this is transformational, I'm so excited.'*

'I feel like a new person,' said Matt.

'I know how you all feel. I think we all feel the same,' said Isabella.

'Well, before I give you the tenth step, please share with the group which step was your biggest breakthrough.'

'That's easy,' said Matt. *'Step Five, believe in yourself. I'm not fully there yet but I'm heading in the right direction thanks to all of you.'*

'For me,' said Brianna, *'it was Step Two – what is your life all about? It made me really look within myself and dig deep. I had got into a rut, a routine of just existing, working and paying bills. Now I know my life is about evolving to be the best me I can be. I'm just so excited about my future, I feel good inside. Thank you so much Michael for letting me be part of the team and sharing the Ten Steps. Thank you.'*

'I can't accept the thanks, it has to go to the voice, to our higher power that shared these Ten Steps with us, for me I thank God again. You decide your beliefs. How about you Ade?'

'I've just been thinking since you asked the question there is not one step that stands out. I just loved all of them, and the journey to this point and I'm looking forward to the tenth step if you will ever tell us, Michael,' Ade said with a smile.

Lian said, *'Mine was Step Eight – accepting responsibility. I think this is what's held me back. I accept responsibility for my kids but nothing else... watch this space!'* Ade looked at Lian. *'What does that mean, Lian. Am I in trouble?'* he said with a smile while squeezing her hand. *'No, I'm just going to be a better all-round person, and we, as a couple and family, are shooting for the moon.'*

'What's yours, Michael?' Isabella said.

'Mine is Step One. When the voice questioned me and asked me 'Who are you?' That was my wake-up call to accept where I am today as a new beginning and not an end. How about you Isabella?'

'Mine is the tenth step...'

'What, you know already?' said Matt.

'Of course she knows, she's Michael's wife!' Brianna spoke with a smile on her face.

'Do you want me to tell you now or do you want the cheesecake first?' I said with a grin.

There was a resounding *'Now!'* from the team.

'The tenth step **is to share your blessings. The voice said I have blessed you with this information to be a blessing not just to yourself but also to others. You were born to win, and it is now time to share your winnings.**

'Did you get that? You were born to win – not to be mediocre, not to just survive, not to just be ok, but to win, and part of that winning is helping others win. You see, we are all born to win, but that doesn't mean we are going to win. It means we have what it takes, but it will take the Ten Steps to get you to start winning. You were not made ordinary, you were made extraordinary. You have unique DNA. There is only one of you in the world. You are very special Born to Win. It's time to start winning the game of life.

'I challenge you to start winning and to share your blessings.

'Think about how we all feel right now. Imagine if I hadn't shared the Ten Steps and just kept them to myself. None of you would be any wiser or feel the way you feel now.'

'That would have been selfish,' said Matt.

'You are absolutely right,' I said, 'to not go out and share the Ten Steps is a crime wouldn't you agree?'

'Yes, that's a crime to humanity,' Ade responded.

'You see, the true gift of life and fulfilment is when you help others. Not just giving them money but giving them tools to become the best person they can be.

'If we change people for the better, we can change the world. Yes, together, we can change the world, one person at a time.

'We can be an instrument for change – good or bad. I choose GOOD. You can become successful while helping many others to become successful. Remember, we defined success as not just money or material things, success as a person.

'The world was full of so many people who had the answers but didn't share them. The world is changing, and social media gives us so much access to information. In some cases, information overload. You could have received the Ten Steps as an email or a video on YouTube! They are great channels to build your wealth of knowledge, but they cannot replace the old-fashioned experience we have had by working as a small team, wouldn't you agree?'

I had the attention of the whole team. They all nodded in agreement.

'Here is the challenge you all have to do, and this also includes me. In the next two weeks, you have to start a new group of your own with a maximum of six people or a minimum of three people, including yourself.

'You see, by working within a new team, you get the most out of it, and your chance of success is very high. Me leading this group made me more account-able, and it helped me understand the Ten Steps better and implement them.

'If you don't start a team of your own, you won't grow because the power is in the sharing – unless you don't want to grow? That's your choice. I can't always be there for you, but you can be there for yourself.'

Isabella butted in, *'Now you understand why I chose the tenth step for me. It was because I saw Michael transform and change every day before my very eyes, and that's because of you guys. I know that Michael knows that if he didn't have the group discussions, preparations, anxiety – yes, he was anxious most days before the meetings – he wouldn't be where he is today and would have easily strayed away from the Ten Steps. I'm already making a list of people that I'm going to ask if they want to be part of my* **'born to win' class and explore their potential.***'*

I looked at Isabella. She was glowing, and there was a vibrancy within her that I hadn't seen for years.

'I love you,' I mouthed to her silently. She smiled at me, and the little crinkle on her nose and in the corners of her eyes told me that she loved me too, and we were going to make it.

'So team, first you have to decide if you want to be an instrument for change or just keep it to yourself. I don't need to know, that's your decision. I have done my part, it's up to you now. If you do want to set up a group I am here for you, but let's do that on a one on one basis.'

'This sounds like the end of us,' said Matt.

'No, it isn't. It's the beginning of us. We will still meet, chat, share successes, but we need to expand this information. We are a team. I think we should meet once a month or every other month for dinner, and we can take it in turns.'

Everyone agreed that this was a great idea.

'Just one point of caution. Getting a team to work the Ten Steps with you means facing rejection. Do you remember what happened in the beginning and how Tom ridiculed us? Well, that's going to happen again and again. There are people out there that are just not interested. Some are negative. They are deaf to change and transformation. You know what I mean, so the key is to be able to say "no" to someone if you don't feel they want to learn or change. It's not how good the teacher is; it's how good the student is that makes a difference. That's why we have done such great work together. We are all good students. Remember, a good student is someone who listens, learns and applies. They put what they learned into action.

"That's what the tenth step is about – putting what we have learned into action and sharing.

'Remember the serious conversation I had with Matt, but he was so glad that I did? As the voice said, many call, but only a few listen. This process of sharing is to be enjoyed, not stressful, so don't force yourself on people... don't work with someone who is not a good student. Share a little information and see if they are interested. Again remember you got interested because you noticed a change in me. That's the key – you bless yourself, you change, and your friends and family will want to know why. Then you select the ones you want but no more than six people.

'Is everyone good with this?'

They all nodded in agreement.

'Oh dear, I forgot the cheesecake! Lian, Isabella and I will clear the table. Can you cut a slice of cheesecake for everyone, please?'

Lian made excellent cheesecakes. She had undoubtedly mastered the art of baking.

'Before we finish tonight does anyone have any questions?'

'Yes, I do. When will we meet again?' Matt said.

'Well, I think we all need some space as it's been intense these last ten days, but how about we meet a week from now at the Rose & Crown where we all started?'

Everyone agreed that was a great idea. We thanked each other for the support, and Ade told us that he felt that life was really good – it's just down to per-spective. He felt that he was partially blind but could now see again.

We all agreed with him that was how every one of us felt, also.

With that, we all said our goodbyes, hugged each other. Then once everyone had left, we did a quick tidy up. Isabella and I poured another glass of wine. It was a great evening, and it had been a significant life-changing ten days. Now the work begins… **Do I have the discipline to follow through? I thought.**

'Isabella, I will need your help. We need to hold each other accountable going forward and stay disciplined to our action plan.'

'Of course, Michael, we are a new team now' We looked into each other's eyes… 'I love you, Michael,' she said. 'I love you so much, Isabella.' With that, we kissed each other and went to bed.

Tomorrow is another new day of possibilities.

Please scan the QR code to download the companion
workbook that is included with this book.

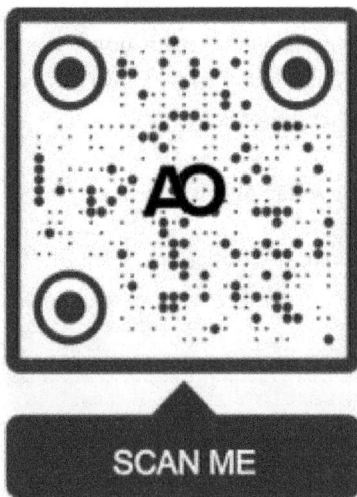

www.ingramcontent.com/pod-product-compliance
Lightning Source LLC
LaVergne TN
LVHW041252080426
835510LV00009B/704